THE CHURCH IN
EXILE

THE CHURCH IN
EXILE

GOD'S COUNTERCULTURE
IN A NON-CHRISTIAN WORLD

Revised Edition

JAMES W.
THOMPSON

LEAFWOOD
PUBLISHERS

THE CHURCH IN EXILE

God's Counterculture in a Non-Christian World

Copyright 2010 by James W. Thompson

ISBN 978-0-89112-273-9
LCCN 2010032116

Printed in the United States of America

Scripture quotations, unless otherwise noted, are from The Holy Bible, New International
Version. Copyright 1984, International Bible Society. Used by permission of Zondervan
Publishers. Scripture quotations noted NRSV are taken from the New Revised Standard
Version Bible, copyright 1989, Division of Christian Education of the National Council of
the Churches of Christ in the United States of America. Used by permission. All rights
reserved. Scripture quotations noted RSV are taken from the Revised Standard Version of
the Bible, copyright 1952 [2nd edition, 1971] by the Division of Christian Education of
the National Council of the Churches of Christ in the United States of America. Used by
permission. All rights reserved.

LIBRARY OF CONGRESS CATALOGING-IN-PUBLICATION DATA
Thompson, James, 1942-
 The church in exile : God's counter-culture in a non-Christian world / James W.
Thompson. -- Rev. ed.
     p. cm.
 ISBN 978-0-89112-643-0
 1. Christianity--20th century. 2. Bible. N.T. Peter, 1st--Criticism, interpretation, etc. I. Title.
II. Title: God's counter-culture in a non-Christian world.
 BR121.3.T45 2010
 270.8'2--dc22

                                                                    2010032116

Cover design by Rick Gibson
Interior text design by Sandy Armstrong

Leafwood Publishers is an imprint of
Abilene Christian University Press.
1626 Campus Court
Abilene, Texas 79601
1-877-816-4455 toll free

For current information about all Leafwood titles, visit our Web site:
www.leafwoodpublishers.com

                    15 14 13 12 11 10 / 6 5 4 3 2 1

CONTENTS

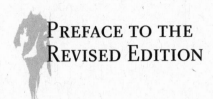

PREFACE TO THE REVISED EDITION

I read recently of a group of English teenagers who heard the story of the birth of Jesus for the first time. After listening with great interest to one of the most familiar narratives of the Bible, one of the teenagers exclaimed, "It's a great story. But why did they give the baby a curse word for his name?" This incident occurred in the part of the world that was once called Christendom, a place where the story of Jesus was known everywhere.

Many of us have watched with dismay as the world of Christendom has disappeared. With its disappearance came a loss of Christian influence in public life, the decline of church membership, and deterioration of traditional moral standards. These changes have left Christians disoriented and wondering how to respond. I first wrote *The Church in Exile* twenty years ago as I observed these changes and discovered valuable answers to our dilemma in 1 Peter, a little epistle nestled near the back of the New Testament. Few of us had paid much attention to this letter until we rediscovered its message for "aliens and exiles" (1 Pet. 2:11).

Recognizing that those who live after Christendom are also exiles, we discovered that an ancient letter spoke powerfully to our own time. Since I wrote *The Church in Exile*, committed Christians have become further marginalized in an increasingly secularized culture. I am convinced that our challenge is not to recover the lost days of an entire society shaped by Christian influence, but to be lights in the world, uniting with the first Christian exiles and countless others around the world today who live faithfully in the context of public apathy or hostility.

I am grateful to Leafwood Publishers for the release of this revised edition. I hope that *The Church in Exile* will stimulate discussion and, like the epistle of 1 Peter, provide encouragement for exiles.

James W. Thompson
August 2010

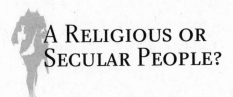

Chapter 1

A Religious or Secular People?

"To the exiles of the Dispersion. . . ."
1 Peter 1:1-2

"We are a religious people," Justice William O. Douglas once wrote about Americans.[1] Evidence to support his conclusion can be found everywhere, both in our history and in our present situation. When Alexis de Tocqueville visited America in the first half of the nineteenth century, he noted that religion was "the foremost of the political institutions" of America.[2] American presidents, from Washington to George W. Bush, have spoken in religious terms in a way that amazes the people of other countries. When President Dwight Eisenhower said in 1954, "Our government makes no sense unless it is founded on a deeply felt religious faith,"[3] he gave expression to what most public officials believed.

Evidence that we are a "religious people" can still be found when one compares American religious practice with the religious expression of the citizens of other western countries. The percentage of Americans who believe in God, pray, and attend church regularly is the highest of any advanced western country.

9

According to a survey conducted in 2007, more than ninety-six percent of Americans say that they believe in God or a higher power.[4] More than fifty percent of Americans say that religion is very important in their lives.[5] Although the percentage of Muslims in America has increased significantly, the Gallup Poll reported in 2009 that almost eight in ten Americans identify themselves as Christian.[6] School children throughout the nation still recite the Pledge of Allegiance, with its words about "one nation under God."

Many of us are undoubtedly surprised, even incredulous, to hear that "we are a religious people," for we see an enormous amount of evidence to the contrary. Indeed, we have witnessed startling changes in the place that religion holds in our society. These changes are particularly apparent in public education. The litigation and debate over prayer in the public schools reflect the movement that has taken place in our society. In past generations, the public schools were heavily influenced by Protestantism, and this influence was noted in the place commonly given to Bible reading and prayer, the schools' mission of building character, and the forum that was often given to local ministers. Within the past several decades, however, religion has been in full retreat in public education. Under the present interpretation of the Establishment Clause of the First Amendment, any public discussion of religion in our lives is often considered inappropriate. Thus, courses in values may be taught, but no preference may be given to Christian values. Courses in sex education or marriage and family life may be taught, but they include no indication that important religious values are involved in shaping one's own lifestyle. One analysis of textbooks has pointed out that grade school American history texts give the impression that religion virtually ceased to exist after the Puritans. Abolitionists are mentioned, but their religious motives are not.[7] The great religious revivals of the nineteenth century commonly go unmentioned.

No one who watches our entertainment would get the impression that "we are a religious people." The constant barrage of television programming depicting assaults on Christian morality would be impossible without a market. Portrayals of adultery and casual sex would not be consistently given in the movies and on television if the public did not accept this behavior. Producers offer material that conflicts with the Christian view of the world simply because a huge market for it exists in our society.

These changes may suggest that the "religion" that is prominent in our society is only a thin veneer over a fundamentally secular culture, and that we are no longer a religious people. If we are no longer a religious society, Christians now face an urgent question: How do we live faithfully in a world where the Christian faith is no longer a significant part of our national culture? To live faithful lives is no challenge when we are surrounded by neighbors and friends who share our values. When everyone at the office or in the neighborhood shares our values, we can be Christians and still be conformed to the world around us. But when Christians become such a minority group that their behavior appears odd or even absurd, they face a severe test.

How do Christians respond to this new situation where strong Christian convictions are no longer a part of the mainstream of our society? Many Christians are struggling with that question today. The strategy of a significant number of religious people in the past decade has been to attempt to bring religion back to the place it once occupied in public life. In the closing decades of the twentieth century, the Moral Majority, for example, advocated the reintroduction of prayer and Bible reading into the public schools. Others have attempted to introduce textbooks to schools that are considered more compatible with the Bible. I am convinced that these strategies are doomed to fail because they depend on a public that holds strong Christian convictions. If the public is no longer Christian, we will never bring religious observance back to the prominent place it once had. Christians now belong to a distinctly minority group. Our behavior will increasingly be considered strange to the majority of the population. This new situation presents Christians with a severe test—on the job, at school, and in our relationships with neighbors. We are now discovering the challenge of being Christians when it is not popular to be a Christian.

First Peter: A Letter to Strangers and Aliens

If we have now discovered that Christian faith makes us strangers in our own land, we will do well to recall that early Christianity did not come into existence in the midst of public favor. Nor did it grow because it was popular and easily accepted. If we are now discovering that our Christianity places us in a minority group, we find ourselves in a situation similar to that faced by the early Christians. During the first four centuries, Christians met in small house churches surrounded by neighbors and family members who scorned their beliefs and their morality. Thus, in our attempts to learn how to live the Christian life in a non-Christian society, we will learn from the earliest Christians how to live when others do not share our values.

The epistle of 1 Peter is addressed to "exiles of the Dispersion in Pontus, Galatia, Cappadocia, Asia and Bithynia" (1:1) sometime in the latter half of the first century. The first words of the epistle provide a graphic view of the problems faced by these communities.

The people are "the exiles of the Dispersion." The description of Christians as "exiles" is a reminder of their status as a minority group within their culture. Throughout history, the exile has lived a vulnerable existence. In the twenty-first century, the fate of the exile is the continuing source of international tension and war, for exiles commonly suffer discrimination and mistreatment. They find themselves cut off from their homeland and scorned where they live. They are the objects of discrimination, and often of persecution. Often they do not blend in with the larger society because of the color of their skin, their language, religion, or customs. In ancient times, exiles were also victimized when they did not blend in with their society. The author of Hebrews recalled that Abraham "sojourned . . . as in a foreign land, living in tents . . ." (11:9), and that the great heroes of the faith were "strangers and exiles on the earth" (11:13). Those exiles constantly suffered abuse because, as a minority group, they did not fit in where they lived.

According to 1 Peter, Christians are exiles. The Christian life is not unlike that of the Israelites in Egypt or Babylon, who also did not assimilate into the larger population. The theme of the exile existence runs throughout 1 Peter. The author speaks in 1:17 of the "time of your exile." In 2:11, the readers are addressed as "aliens and exiles." As people who had left the "traditions of their fathers" (1:18), they were greeted by the hostility and suspicion that are normally reserved for a foreign community. Thus they knew the pressure, the discrimination, and the fear of living in a strange land.

The "alien" Christians who first read 1 Peter were not strangers in their own lands because of their skin colors or their nationalities. Their obedience to the call of Christ had made them exiles. Unlike those who are exiles because of their ethnic backgrounds, these Christians could have ceased being exiles simply by blending in with the larger population.

The problems that faced this minority group of Christians were common throughout the ancient world. In the second century, an unknown writer wrote a defense of Christianity for a pagan audience in which he said:

> For Christians cannot be distinguished from the rest of the human race by country or language or customs. They do not live in cities of their own; they do not use a peculiar form of speech; they do not follow an eccentric manner of life. This doctrine of theirs has not been discovered by the ingenuity or deep thought of inquisitive men, nor do they put forward a merely human teaching, as some people do. Yet, although they live in Greek and barbarian cities alike, as each man's lot has been cast, and follow the customs of the country in clothing and food and other matters of daily living, at the same time they give proof of the remarkable and admittedly extraordinary constitution of their own commonwealth. They live in their own countries, but only as aliens.[8]

The writer proceeds to demonstrate what made Christians aliens in their own lands. He focuses on the Christian morality, which separates them from their neighbors. Undoubtedly the readers of 1 Peter were exiles because of their new moral commitments. They were discovering that it was costly to be a Christian.

The word "dispersion," which is used in 1 Peter 1:1 (cf. James 1:1) to describe Christians, suggests both the isolation of Christians from each other and the common bond that they shared with people in distant places. The word "dispersion" had been commonly used for Jews who had been scattered throughout the Near East. Those who lived in the dispersion knew that, while they were scattered into tiny isolated communities, they were part of a worldwide people, and they looked forward to their ultimate reunification with the people of God. The word was a reminder for Christians that, although they were a tiny minority group in their own cities, they were a part of a worldwide community.

The fact that they belonged to a larger company of people is also indicated in the fact that they are the exiles of "Pontus, Galatia, Cappadocia, Asia, and Bithynia" (1:1). These are provinces in a vast area comprising almost the whole of Asia Minor, a place where overland travel was hazardous at best. That there were congregations there at all in the latter half of the first century is a testimony to the power of Christianity. Even more remarkable is the apparent solidarity of Christians in these distant places with each other. All of them could be addressed in one letter, and all of them faced a similar situation: the challenge of living their Christian lives as exiles in their own lands.

Exile Communities Yesterday

The epistle of 1 Peter has spoken with special power whenever people have discovered that their faith has made them exiles. The epistle spoke with special power during the Third Reich. During Easter week of 1945, Dietrich Bonhoeffer led his fellow prisoners in worship at the prison camp at Schonberg, where he had been a constant source of encouragement. He read from 1 Peter 1:3, "Blessed be the God and Father of our Lord Jesus Christ! By his great mercy we have been born anew to a living hope through the resurrection of Jesus Christ from the dead. . . ." After Bonhoeffer had spoken for a few minutes on the meaning of those ancient words for their situation, the prison doors opened and two sinister men entered the cell and said, "Prisoner Bonhoeffer, get ready to come with us." Everyone knew what those words meant. Bonhoeffer went to his execution on the cold day of April 9, 1945. He had found a special meaning to 1 Peter in that situation.[9]

Martin Niemoller was imprisoned in Berlin because he rejected the interference of the Nazis in the affairs of the Protestant Church. Under Nazi pressure, the German church had passed a resolution barring anyone with Jewish ancestry from being ordained to the ministry. Niemoller resisted the Nazi pressure and openly spoke out against the resolution. He wrote to his wife from prison: "We do not want to forget that even the German fatherland means a foreign exile to us, as for the man who had nothing as he lay in the manger because he laid down his head out of love for the people."[10] Perhaps his realization that one can be an exile in his own land came from a reading of 1 Peter.

The epistle of 1 Peter spoke with such power to the victims of Nazi persecution that they recognized that the distance between Europe in the twentieth century and Asia Minor in the first century was not great at all. They discovered that, although 1 Peter was originally addressed to the "exiles of the Dispersion in Pontus, Galatia, Cappadocia, Asia, and Bithynia," it also spoke to Berlin, Frankfurt, Munich, Stuttgart, and any other community where Christians discovered that they have become exiles in their own land.

Exile Communities Today

Does 1 Peter speak also to Christians in Dallas, Atlanta, Los Angeles, and Chicago early in the twenty-first century? This epistle was written for exiles, and only those who have experienced exile for their faith are likely to feel that they are addressed by it. If our Christian faith makes us exiles, we are not likely to experience it in the form that it took during the Third Reich, for we are not likely to experience persecution from a hostile government. Nevertheless, there are other ways of being Christian exiles.

The changes that have taken place within the last generation will not make exiles of those whose Christian commitment demands little of them. Nor will it make exiles of churches that speak only to echo what others are already saying. Indeed, religion may remain popular in our culture as long as it exists only to bless the popular values. However, those who are willing to say that God has decisively revealed himself only in Jesus Christ, and that our response to him is a matter of ultimate importance, will be exiles in a culture that believes that all commitments are equally valid. In a world where we choose "alternate lifestyles," each of which is equally appropriate, those whose lifestyles are shaped by the one who sacrificed himself for others will be exiles in their own country. In a culture where we are expected to keep ourselves free of binding commitments, those who bind themselves to others in marriage or in the church community will also be exiles. Thus we face the task of living out our Christian lives, as did the early Christians, as exiles in our own land. Like the exiles of every age, we discover that it is an insecure existence to live as a minority group surrounded by those who think our beliefs are absurd.

How do we find the resources to live as exiles? The epistle of 1 Peter is a sermon that was preached to offer such resources. Indeed, the writer's numerous references to the "new birth" (1:3, 23), baptism (3:21), and the new life (1:14) may suggest that the readers were new Christians who were experiencing the exile existence after their conversion. In the introductory words of the epistle (1:1-2), he offers a hint of two major resources in the Christian life. In the first place, the exiles recall that they are the *elect* exiles "according to the foreknowledge of God." That is, they were neither the victims of an unfortunate set of circumstances nor the objects of pity, for they had been "chosen" or "elected" by God as surely as ancient Israel had been chosen and loved by God. Their world may look upon them with scorn and reject them, but God has *chosen* them. This reminder will give them strength for their journey into unknown circumstances.

In the second place, the introduction closes with a blessing: "Grace and peace be multiplied." They are not dependent upon their own resources, but on the grace of God. Whatever fears of circumstances beyond their control might disturb them, they knew that they could rely on the grace of God.

This letter of encouragement finally concludes with Peter's words in 5:12, "By Silvanus, a faithful brother as I regard him, I have written briefly to you, exhorting and declaring that this is the true grace of God; stand firm in it." At the beginning and end of this letter, the readers are reminded that times of trial will be the special occasions when they will discover the "true grace of God." If Christians from ancient Asia Minor could find the grace of God and a word of encouragement for their exile existence, Christians in the twenty-first century will also discover that "the true grace of God" is experienced when we live faithful lives in the midst of adversity.

NOTES

1 Quoted in Richard John Neuhaus, *The Naked Public Square* (Grand Rapids: Eerdmans, 1984), 80.

2 Paul Johnson, "The Almost-Chosen People," in Richard John Neuhaus, ed., *Unsecular America* (Grand Rapids: Eerdmans, 1986), 10.

3 Ibid., 9, 10.

4 Rodney Stark, *What Americans Really Believe* (Waco: Baylor University Press, 2008), 117.

5 http://pewforum.org/How-Religious-Is-Your-State-.aspx

6 http://www.gallup.com/video/117394/Christianity-Slow-Decline.aspx

7 George Marsden, "Are Secularists the Threat?" in Neuhaus, *Unsecular America*, p. 45.

8 *Epistle to Diognetus*, 5:1-5.

9 William Willimon, *The Gospel for the Person Who Has Everything* (Valley Forge: Judson, 1978), 59.

10 *Exile in the Fatherland*, ed. Hubert G. Locke (Grand Rapids: Eerdmans, 1986), 124.

Questions for Discussion

1. Describe some of the changes in your lifetime in society's common acceptance of Christian values.

2. What references to God or to the Bible do you recall that were made by public officials? Can you see evidence of changing values?

3. What evidence for a changing moral climate do you see on television? Does television reflect values or promote certain values?

4. To what extent do Christian convictions pose difficulties in becoming successful in the marketplace? In the professions?

5. In light of your answers to questions 1-4, to what extent are we living as exiles (i.e., Are we at an appropriate level of non-conformity to the culture of which we are a part)?

6. What resources for living as exiles are to be seen in the first two verses of 1 Peter?

7. Do certain parts of the Bible speak with special power at different times in history? What themes in 1 Peter give it a special meaning today? What parallels can we see between then and now?

7. What significance can we find in the fact that these exiles could all be addressed in one letter, even though they were separated by hundreds of miles?

Chapter 2

Born Again

"By his great mercy we have been born anew. . . ."
1 Peter 1:3-12

During the 1976 presidential campaign, the major newspapers and news magazines commissioned their reporters to cover the new religious phenomenon of "born again Christians." The media were familiar with various expressions of Christianity, but the "born again" type was totally new to many. It had been brought to public attention by a candidate who was a "born again Christian." Jimmy Carter's religion became a major issue in the news.

Later, when the television preachers were shaken by scandal, the *New York Times* published a glossary of religious terms for the benefit of the wider audience. Religious terms had to be explained to the wider public as if they were foreign words in need of translation. Common Christian expressions—new birth, salvation by faith, the grace of God—belong only to little subcultures speaking a language unknown to the general public.

The readers of 1 Peter were conscious of having been "born anew," and they belonged to a tiny subculture in Asia Minor.

Indeed, because their existence as "born again" Christians is mentioned three times in the letter (1:3, 23; 2:2), 1 Peter is widely regarded as a letter especially for new Christians. Their new birth had separated them from their ancestral roots (1:18) and divided households (2:18; 3:1), leaving them vulnerable and subject to abuse. To be born again in this situation was to leave the security of home and to become an exile in one's own land. This new birth had introduced Christians to considerable pain.

We might expect this situation to elicit from the author some words of consolation for people who could see no end in sight for their difficult circumstances. But the opening words of 1 Peter catch us by surprise, for they are a song of praise! We expect songs of praise in the context of good news. We are not surprised to see songs of praise in the Bible in moments of triumph and celebration, as in the opening chapters of Luke's Gospel, for there people break into singing because of the news that God has brought tidings of joy. But in 1 Peter the subject is the alienation and suffering that Christians experience. In the original language, 1 Peter 1:3-12 is one long sentence connected by a series of parallel phrases. That is, 1:3-12 is like a song of praise and thanksgiving. Whereas most epistles begin with a brief expression of thanksgiving, 1 Peter begins with a lengthy song of praise. Some writers have suggested that these words were part of a celebratory hymn that was sung at baptism.

Sometimes how writers say something is as important as what they say. Writers turn to poetry and singing at times to express what cannot be expressed in prose. Feelings of joy and delight have always been set to music. When we recall that the readers of 1 Peter were struggling as exiles, the musical quality of the opening paragraph is astonishing. In a long poetic expression of thanksgiving that sets the stage for the rest of the epistle, the opening lines of 1 Peter invite Christians to join in a celebration in song! The new exile existence calls forth not a lament but a song of joy.

The words "blessed be the God and Father of our Lord Jesus Christ" (1:3) are similar to other Jewish expressions of gratitude. They are words of celebration. The Psalmist says: "Blessed be the Lord the God of Israel, who alone does wondrous things" (Ps. 72:18). Zechariah bursts into song at the birth of John the Baptist: "Blessed be the Lord God of Israel, for he has visited and redeemed his people" (Luke 1:68). The Epistle to the Ephesians, like 1 Peter, opens with a song of praise: "Blessed be the God and Father of our Lord Jesus Christ" (1:3). The alien existence is obviously no occasion for sorrow.

The one fact about the new existence that is cause for celebration is the hope Christians experience. "By his great mercy we have been born anew to a living hope by the resurrection of Jesus Christ from the dead, and to an inheritance that is imperishable, undefiled, and unfading, kept in heaven for you" (1:4). The suffering, the trials, and the discrimination are only a minor chord in this epistle, for the major theme is the hope that places suffering in perspective. Before the epistle gives any advice, Peter reminds the readers of their hope. It is the one thing in this world that is permanent. The words about hope seem to gush with synonyms and adjectives: "inheritance . . . imperishable, undefiled and unfading." Without the new birth, there would have been no alien existence, but there would also have been no hope.

This theme is developed later when the readers are told that their "faith and hope are in God" (1:21). In 1:13 Peter challenges them, "Set your hope fully on the grace that is coming to you at the revelation of Jesus Christ." From this hope they acquire the resources for not adapting to the moral standards of their age, for this hope generates moral commitments that are difficult to keep.

When their neighbors ask about their new way of life, they are to "give a reason for the hope that is within them" (1 Pet. 3:15). Undoubtedly, without this hope they would not have the capacity to endure the discrimination and other aspects of the alien existence. The promise that comes at the conclusion of the book—that after a "little while" God will "restore, establish, and strengthen" them (1 Pet. 5:10)—placed their suffering in a new perspective.

It may be ironical that the one community in the ancient world that possessed hope was the one where people suffered for their faith. Hopelessness apparently reigned among the secure people who adapted easily to their environment. Indeed, the pre-Christian life of the Ephesians is described as "without hope" and "without God" (2:12). The Thessalonians are reminded that others "have no hope" (1 Thess. 4:13). Their pagan neighbors could imagine no future. Some of them believed that their lives were controlled by fate. Others chose a life devoted to pleasure because they had no hope. Gilbert Murray described the message to humanity that was offered by some of the Greek thinkers of that time: "Fear nothing, desire nothing, possess nothing, and then Life, with all its ingenuity of malice, cannot disappoint you."[1] Christians, however, knew of the resurrection of Christ (1 Pet. 1:3). This story was the source of hope and the basis for the conviction that "an inheritance which is imperishable, undefiled, and unfading, kept in heaven" awaits us (1 Pet. 1:4).

Hope Today

Christians in the twenty-first century, like the original readers of 1 Peter, live in a culture marked by hopelessness. Christopher Lasch, in his important book, *The Culture of Narcissism: American*

Life in an Age of Diminishing Expectations, describes the hopelessness of our time. In contrast to earlier stages of our civilization on this continent, when people believed that every year would bring greater prosperity and new scientific breakthroughs to prolong lives, we now suffer from deep anxiety about the future. Our fears about the future are kept alive with the grim reminders in each day's news about trends that are beyond our control. More and more studies suggest that our industrial economy is doing irreparable damage to our environment. Other studies point toward an inevitable financial collapse under the burden of an uncontrolled national debt. Today we are worried about the future of our environment and the possibility that human life cannot continue on this planet. We are also worried that a new epidemic will be uncontrollable.

For many people, the way to cope with the grim prospect of the future is to protect themselves psychologically from the anxieties of the time. Therefore, the answer is to expect nothing and not be disappointed.

Many who live for the present moment have given up their hopes because they have been disappointed in the past by unrealized hopes. During the past generation, we have seen a variety of hopes that came to nothing. Some people worked to eliminate poverty or the threat of war. Some got involved in the political process, thinking that their efforts could improve the quality of life or lead to the reduction of tensions in the world, only to recognize that their hopes were like mirages that disappeared.

If we give up our expectations for the future, we cease believing that it is worthwhile to become involved in the community or to support important causes. If we expect nothing, we are most likely to cultivate our own personal pleasures, retreating into the little private world of the self. The conspicuous consumption that is associated with our time may in fact be a symptom of hopelessness, for those who want everything now have given up on the future. This hopelessness is the source of the narcissism described by Christopher Lasch. He says: "After the political turmoil of the sixties, Americans have retreated to purely personal preoccupations. Having no hope of improving their lives in any of the ways that matter, people have convinced themselves that what matters is psychic self-improvement: getting in touch with their feelings, eating health food, taking lessons in ballet or belly-dancing, immersing themselves in the wisdom of the East, jogging, learning how to 'relate,' overcoming the 'fear of pleasure.'"[2] He adds that these pursuits may be harmless in themselves, but that they reflect our loss of hope in the future.

The Christian who is "born again to a living hope" is likely to possess a commodity that is missing in our culture. Even today, this hope will make us strangers in a culture that has lost its hope.

This hope is not to be confused with the age-old optimism which believes that "every day in every way" things are getting better. The remarkable fact about 1 Peter is that this letter actually celebrates Christian hope in a context where the readers had no reason to believe in progress! All that was visible to their eyes was the hostility of their neighbors and the prospect of "suffering as a Christian" (4:16). David Kendall has said: "It is one thing to have and to herald hope when we are well fed, financially secure, comfortably related to family and friends, and appropriately admired by professional and personal peers. It is quite another thing, however, to possess and to proclaim hope in a situation where comfort and convenience are out of the question and where alienation and affliction are the order of the day."[3]

The hope expressed in 1 Peter is not that of a person whose future is made secure by his adaptability to the environment in which he lives. This hope is expressed against the background of the hard realities of affliction and alienation.

The Present Joy

If we are impressed by the fact that 1 Peter begins with a celebration of hope in the midst of stress and alienation, we are equally surprised that the opening lines of 1 Peter abound in expressions of joy. Twice in the opening paragraph of 1 Peter, the readers are reminded of the joy of their Christian life. "In this you rejoice," Peter says (1:6). He describes a life in which they "rejoice with unutterable and exalted joy" (1:8). One might have assumed that joy was the possession of the majority culture, whose lives were devoted to "licentiousness, passions, drunkenness, revels, carousing and lawless idolatry" (4:4). Indeed, an observer of the early Christians might have assumed that the Christians, by remaining aloof from the pagan celebrations, were missing out on the joy of that civilization. While their pagan neighbors were enjoying the present, Christians were the victims of slander and oppression.

How could the Christians "rejoice with unutterable and exalted joy" in this climate? Was it because they refused to see the world as it is? According to 1 Peter, the Christians were under no illusions about their situation. "In this you rejoice," they are told, "though now for a little while you may have to suffer various trials" (1:6). The genuineness of their faith is tested by fire, as they face the hostility of their neighbors. When they can see nothing but the trials that their new faith has brought on them, they rejoice in the presence of a harsh reality. They, and not their neighbors, are rejoicing.

One of the old criticisms of Christianity is that Christians took the joy out of life and replaced it with an emphasis on sorrow, pain, and suffering. According to 1 Peter, however, Christians can experience genuine joy in the midst of suffering because the resurrection hope (1:3) has made us aware that even "when we do not see him" we believe in him and "rejoice with him with unutterable and exalted joy" (1:8). Even when we cannot see anything but the suffering, the resurrection hope enables us to believe in the future.

In 1 Peter 4:13, the readers are encouraged to "rejoice in so far as you share Christ's sufferings, that you may also rejoice and be glad when his glory is revealed." That is, the ultimate rejoicing comes at the end when our faith becomes sight. The joy we experience at the moment is an anticipation of the future, the experience of one who looks forward so much to the future that he already feels its presence.

During World War II, those who struggled in the resistance recall the change in mood that came when they received the news on their clandestine radios that the allies had landed and were on the path that would bring liberation. For the moment, the dangers for the resistance fighters had not changed, for they still lived in a hostile environment. But the knowledge that liberation was certain made their efforts worthwhile. They soon realized that those in power were the ones who lived in fear, and that they themselves already had reason to celebrate. The good news for them, which still lay in the future, was already being felt.

The joy of 1 Peter has grown out of the certainty of the future and the knowledge that the future was already breaking in on the Christians. Despite the trials, the Christians could recognize that the present moment was the turning point in history, a moment that had only been dreamed of by their predecessors.

The prophets who prophesied of the grace that was to be yours searched and inquired about this salvation; they inquired what person or time was indicated by the Spirit of Christ within them when predicting the sufferings of Christ and the subsequent glory. It was revealed to them that they were serving not themselves but you, in the things which have now been announced to you by those who preached the good news to you through the Holy Spirit sent from heaven, things into which angels long to look. (1:10-12)

Their neighbors might look on the Christians with scorn, but they knew that they were living in a time that even the prophets and the angels wished to see. Despite the hostility, it was not a time for condolences. It was a time for celebration, for just beyond them was the future God had prepared for them. Unfortunately, their neighbors could not see it.

What Are We Celebrating?

Helmut Thielicke once observed that the joy we see in our own culture, especially that associated with special occasions like New Year's, is often a manufactured joy that only covers up the emptiness of our lives. Do "noisy New Year's Eve sprees, with their alcoholic dulling of the consciousness, . . . have their origin in our desire to drown out this sound of time which suddenly grows louder at the turn of the year?" he asks. Then he says: "There is a kind of joking that covers up and represses a deeper anxiety or an unsolved problem in our life. Every one of you has had the experience of being depressed or even in despair and saying to yourself, 'Well, there's only one thing for it, cost what it may,

I'll have to find something to make me laugh.' And you went to a movie which you were told was really sidesplitting. And you really did laugh at some of the comical situations. But, lurking in the background, never entirely forgotten, the sadness and the unresolved problem remained."[4]

When Christians refused to participate in the drunken celebrations of their neighbors, they did not take the joy out of life. They had found a joy that was not manufactured, but one rooted in the overwhelming experience of knowing that God has come into our world with good news, and that we are allowed to share in it, believing that God has provided "a salvation ready to be revealed at the last time" (1:5). God's aliens have a cause for celebration.

NOTES

1   Gilbert Murray, *Five Stages of Greek Religion* (New York: Doubleday, 1955), 89, cited in Douglas Hall, "Beyond Cynicism and Credulity: On the Meaning of Christian Hope," *Princeton Seminary Bulletin* 3 (1985), 202.

2   Christopher Lasch, *The Culture of Narcissism: American Life in the Age of Diminishing Expectations* (New York: W. W. Norton, 1978), 4.

3   David W. Kendall, "On Christian Hope," *Interpretation* 41 (1987), 66.

4   Helmut Thielicke, *Christ and the Meaning of Life* (New York: Harper, 1962), 32.

Questions for Discussion

1. What evidence in the first two chapters suggests that the epistle is written for new Christians?

2. Compare the introduction of 1 Peter with the introduction to other epistles, especially 2 Corinthians and Ephesians. How

is the language different from normal prose? Why does 1 Peter begin with this poetic quality?

3. To what extent is Christian hope a common topic in preaching, teaching, and daily conversation? Are Christians distinctive in the way hope has a role in their lives?

4. Page 23 says that "the major theme (of 1 Peter) is the hope which places suffering in perspective." Why is perspective important to the Christian lifestyle? How does our perspective affect us when it is not correctly focused?

5. "Some got involved in the political process ... only to recognize that their hopes were like mirages ..." (p. 25). How does Christian hope change the way we view worldly instruments of change? Does it excuse us from working through these avenues or re-orient our hope to God as the real agent of change?

6. What is the relationship between hope, optimism, and positive thinking?

7. How is the Christian experience of joy distinguished from cultural views of joy?

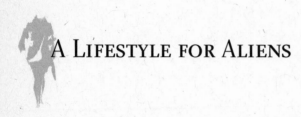

Chapter 3

A Lifestyle for Aliens

"Do not be conformed to the passions of your former ignorance."
1 Peter 1:13-25

"When all become Christians," wrote Jacques Ellul, "the concept of Christianity is void."[1] Students of the history of early Christianity recognize that Ellul's conclusion rests on good historical evidence, for the growth of Christianity resulted in the formation of Christian cultures, Christian societies, and even a Christian world, known as Christendom. The more the church reached the masses, the less Christian it became. As people came to Christianity in greater numbers, the concept of conversion was lost, for they brought with them the ideas and values of their old existence. Thus Christianity was the victim of its own success when conversion lost its original meaning. When everyone became Christian, says Ellul, "they were being required to act as if they were true Christians when very likely they were not."[2]

For more than fifteen hundred years we have lived under Christendom, and we have been reminded that Christendom is not Christianity. In the nineteenth century, Soren Kierkegaard wrote that true Christianity is abolished in a Christian land. "The result of the Christianity of 'Christendom' is that everything, absolutely everything, has remained as it was, only everything has assumed the name 'Christian'—and so (musicians, strike up the tune!) we live a life of paganism."[3] The shocking thing, he wrote, is that "a religion has been abolished by . . . flourishing."[4]

Kierkegaard claimed that the situation was twice as difficult in his day as it was when Christianity came into existence because in Christendom Christianity was confronted, not by pagans and Jews whose strong resentment was aroused, but by people who were made to believe that they were Christians.[5] In his "Christian land," he saw only a Christianity that demanded nothing. It had been altered to fit the tastes of the masses of the people. Such a Christianity dispensed the blessings of salvation, but it demanded no rigorous discipleship. Where Christianity and society were the same, the church existed only to pronounce a blessing on the people without summoning them to repentance and discipleship.

In the earlier part of this century, Dietrich Bonhoeffer saw many of the same problems posed by a Christian land. This Christianity, he said, offered "cheap grace"[6] in the place of authentic discipleship, a Christianity at bargain-basement prices.

The "Christian lands" that Kierkegaard and Bonhoeffer both knew were considerably different from what Americans have experienced. Both of them grew up in state churches in Europe where citizenship and church membership were practically synonymous. Where citizenship and church membership were intertwined, the demands of the gospel were inevitably omitted.

The American experience has been different. The absence of a state church has given religious life a quality that is lacking in the countries where religion and civic life are united. Yet the differences between the United States and European countries may be superficial, for Christendom has included both Europe and North America. As a Christian land, we have experienced the popularity of religion and the periodic times of religious enthusiasm. Yet one may ask, along with Kierkegaard, if this popular Christianity is that of the New Testament and if converts are challenged to live the life that is demanded in the New Testament.

A Call to Holiness

The age of Christendom has come to a close with amazing speed. Within a period of one generation, the pervasive influence of Christianity in our schools, neighborhoods, and civic life has diminished dramatically. Many Christians long had lived under the secure umbrella of a "Christian land" and found their easy Christian assumptions untested. The moral choices made by Christians seemed infinitely easier because a Christian land shared our assumptions about the values of human life, sex and marriage, and many other issues.

Today we face moral decisions under new conditions. The umbrella of a Christian land has been taken away. While we struggle with moral questions, we are bombarded daily with the moral values of a non-Christian land. Having been accustomed to living comfortably within our culture, we are now faced with the task of making choices that may separate us from our culture in a way that we have never before experienced.

Facing moral choices in a non-Christian land requires resources. The epistle of 1 Peter offers an important resource because the recipients of this letter faced problems similar to our own, for they were aliens in their own land also. They too faced moral choices in a culture where their new birth into Christianity had separated them from the values of their land. As aliens in their own land, they were faced with the choice of whether they should blend in with the majority culture or live in such a way that their neighbors would treat them with ridicule and hostility.

Although the epistle begins with celebration and rejoicing (1:3-12), it quickly moves to indicate that there is another side to the Christian life. This side is described in 1:13-21. New birth brings joy and gratitude, according to 1:3-12, but in the new section beginning in 1:13, it involves new commitments.

The first demand of the epistle is to "set your hope fully on the grace that is coming to you at the revelation of Jesus Christ" (1:13). At the end of the paragraph, the writer says, "so that your faith and hope are in God" (1:21). In the opening song that begins the letter, we are reminded that we have been "born anew to a living hope" through the resurrection of Christ (1:3). Before the moral demands are given, we are reminded of our hope, for without hope we would be too defeated to bother with moral commitments. Without hope, we would live for now and blend in with our environment, knowing that we have nothing to do but to "grab the gusto" now.

A vivid image for the intensity of Christian morality is found in the phrase, "Therefore gird up your minds" (1:13, RSV). The expression is literally, "Girding up the loins of your minds." In ancient times one wore the loose-fitting garment around the house, but when the time came for a journey or work in the fields, one "girded up the loins" to prepare for work. In 1 Peter we have the unusual expression, "gird up the loins of your minds." That is, those who have celebrated the joy of God's gifts recognize that the time for work has come. The only response to God's gifts is to prepare for an intense time of labor, one that demands concentration and alertness. Christian morality requires intensity and thoughtfulness.

According to 1 Peter, two alternatives are open to the Christian who lives in an alien land. One may either "be conformed to the passions" of the pre-Christian life or one may "be holy." The Christians are challenged, "Do not be conformed to the passions of your former ignorance, but as he who called you is holy, be holy yourselves in all your conduct" (1:14-15). Apparently the Christian readers had already taken this option, and it had not escaped the notice of their neighbors. Later in the epistle, the author says, "Let the time that is passed suffice for doing what the Gentiles like to do, living in licentiousness, passions, drunkenness, revels, carousing, and lawless idolatry. They are surprised that you do not now join them in the same wild profligacy, and they abuse you" (4:3-4).

The Christians of Asia Minor were not aliens in their own land because of their unusual ethnic origins, their accents, or their dress. Their moral commitments had separated them from the larger populace. Indeed the phrase "they are surprised at you" (4:4) is rendered correctly by the NIV, "They think it strange." The very people who had previously joined their neighbors in their vices had now separated themselves. Thus the author demands that they continue a moral life that is "strange" to the populace.

Perhaps the alienation offered a constant temptation to the Christians to adapt to the environment. Although they have changed, the temptation remains. Consequently, they are warned, "Do not be conformed to the passions of your former ignorance." Later they are reminded that the new lifestyle involves abstaining "from the passions of the flesh that war against the soul" (2:11). Apparently they lived in a world dominated by the passions. When they were redeemed, they were "ransomed from the futile traditions of [their] fathers" (1:18). The new Christian life demanded that they separate from the traditions which glorified the passions.

Elsewhere in the New Testament, we receive frequent reminders that their environment was dominated by the "passions" which are mentioned in 1 Peter. We have a vivid picture in Paul's writings of the moral condition of the world in which Gentile Christians had lived (cf. Rom. 1:24; Eph. 2:3; 1 Thess. 4:5). Especially in Romans 1:18-24 we see Paul's judgment on a pagan world dominated by the passions. He joined his Jewish contemporaries in condemning the sexual indulgence of the ancient culture.

The word rendered "passion" (*epithumia*) commonly has a sexual connotation, and thus it can be translated "lust." New Testament writers assume that Christian communities are surrounded by a world dominated by lust, but they demand that they live by a sexual standard that will amaze their culture. Thus Christians are told not to "be conformed to the passions of your former ignorance." The word for "conform" (*syschematizo*), used also in Romans 12:2, means literally "shape" or "mold." It suggests the image of clay that is being shaped. The author knows how naturally we are shaped by our environment, and thus he calls on Christians not to be shaped by the lusts that dominate their own culture.

We get a vivid impression of what it meant in ancient times to become a Christian from the second-century writer, Justin Martyr, who describes the pilgrimage that he and others made in becoming Christians: "We who formerly rejoiced in uncleanness of life and now love only chastity; we who also used magic arts and have now dedicated ourselves to the good and unbegotten God; we who loved resources of money and possessions more than anything, and now actually share what we have and give to everyone who is in need; we who hated one another and killed one another and would not eat with those of other race, and now since the manifestation of Christ have a common life and pray for our enemies and try to win over those who hate us without just cause."[7]

A Challenge for Today

In a Christian land we might consider it unnecessary to repeat Peter's summons not to be "conformed to the passions" of our culture, for a Christian land would uphold some of our Christian values as a matter of public policy. A Christian land would reinforce the high view of marriage and family that is a part of the Christian heritage. Those values would be inculcated in the schools and in the media and exemplified by the legislative leaders. Indeed, those values were held in esteem and articulated by leaders in an earlier era. Today, however, these values are not articulated as a part of public life. A Christian who is not "conformed to the passions of the flesh" will be, like the Christians of 1 Peter, a stranger and an alien.

Our culture, like that in which the first-century Christians were living, is dominated by lust. One writer said recently that "lust is America's favorite indoor sport."[8] "Lust," according to Henry Fairlie, "is not interested in its partners, but only in gratification of its own craving."[9] It turns people into objects for the satisfaction of an appetite. Lust is different from the romantic love that has been celebrated since the Song of Solomon, and continues to be celebrated in song and fiction. "Falling in love" involves the attraction to the person, as in the Song of Solomon. Lust says, with Dulcinea, in *The Man of La Mancha*, "one pair of arms is like another." Where one goes from one partner to another, it is lust and not love that is predominant.

The media has come to celebrate lust as a way of life, and it bombards us with the message that sex is unrelated to commitment.

TV Guide said in one of its advertisements: "The people who write and produce prime-time television have proven their willingness to tackle every imaginable theme over the past decade. . . . They have moved into areas once considered untouchable in prime time. Yet the most common, most crucial of all themes—the capacity of modern men and women to love, trust, share and provide a moral framework for their children—this seems beyond their grasp."[10]

Elizabeth Achtemeier has written that Hollywood's rapt attention is drawn to sex clubs, switch groups, homosexuals, and triangles, but that "if goodness is found on the human scene, Hollywood is sure it must have come from another planet in the form of E.T. or some equally fanciful figure."[11]

In a Christian land, Christian attitudes toward sex and marriage are nurtured and reinforced. The post-Christian land in which we live is dominated by the lust that encourages casual sexual relationships. Imagine the plight of the Christian man or woman in the university who dares to say that sexual experience and commitment belong together. One can imagine the Christian professional who dares not to participate in this lifestyle. For there are social consequences to such a choice. One immediately becomes a "stranger" or "alien" to others, a visitor from another century.

Christians who find that their moral commitments make them aliens in their own land may perceive this as an unfortunate, if necessary, fate. One may easily feel deprived and lacking in social acceptance because of his Christian morality. If the readers of 1 Peter thought of themselves as deprived, the encouraging letter which they received assured them that their condition was nothing less than a gift. "You were ransomed from the futile ways inherited from your fathers," they are told. They were ransomed, "not with perishable things such as silver or gold, but with the precious blood of Christ, like that of a lamb without blemish or spot" (1:18-19). When they see the moral conditions of their contemporaries, they do not look with envy, nor do they wish to adapt to their moral standards. When they see the environment around them, they know that they have been "ransomed" or set free from the slavery that was involved in ancient morality.

When the ancient Israelites recalled the circumstances of their own pilgrimage, they too recognized that they had been "rescued" in order to discover a new existence. Their "rescue" from Egypt brought a time of hardship in the wilderness, and even moments of homesickness for the security of their former land. Yet they could never forget that they had been "ransomed" by a God who was jealously devoted to them. This God set one major condition for the new relationship: "You shall be holy as I am holy" (Lev. 19:2). Israel was ransomed to be different from her neighbors in order that she might be like God. From this moment on, her life was to be different in its moral shape from the Canaanites and all of the others because of her own relationship with God.

In 1 Peter, the Christian life does not consist only in rejecting the cultural standards of the world around. Christians are to recognize that they are free to be different because they too have been "ransomed" (1:18). To be a Christian is to "be holy as God is holy," the positive alternative to being "conformed to the passions" of one's own culture. Christians are "a holy priesthood" (2:5), a people set apart for a specific mission. If they feel that they are like aliens in their own land, they are not the victims of a cruel misfortune. They are the recipients of a remarkable gift from the God who has set them apart for a new existence.

NOTES

1   Jacques Ellul, *The Subversion of Christianity* (Grand Rapids: Eerdmans, 1986), 35.
2   Ibid., 41.
3   Soren Kierkegaard, *Attack on "Christendom"* (Princeton, N.J.: Princeton University Press, 1968), 164.
4   Ibid., 142.
5   Ibid., 143.
6   Dietrich Bonhoeffer, *The Cost of Discipleship*, 2nd edition (London: SCM Press, 1959), 45.
7   Justin, Apology I.14.
8   Albert Dahlquist, letter to the editor, *Harper's* 276 (February 1988), 11.
9   Henry Fairlie, *The Seven Deadly Sins Today* (Washington, D.C.: New Republic Books, 1978), 175.
10 Elizabeth Achtemeier, *Preaching on Family Relationships* (Philadelphia: Westminster, 1987), 19.
11 Ibid., 20.

Questions for Discussion

1. Comment on the statement that a religion can be abolished by flourishing. If it is possible for a religion to be abolished by flourishing, under what circumstances does this occur? What does this view mean for attempts at church growth where we make the church more attractive to please outsiders?

2. Has America historically belonged to Christendom? How would you define Christendom?

3. To what extent is it useful to become involved in causes that attempt to restore laws that require respect for Christian morality? To what extent are these matters best left to the

church? Do you advocate censorship laws for television and movies?

4. Evaluate the extent to which "cheap grace" is offered within the church? How would you define "cheap grace?"

5. Besides the reference to "passions" in 1 Peter, in what other areas of life does the epistle call for Christians not to be conformed to their environment? Does the church, in its call for moral living, overemphasize sexual sins and give inadequate attention to other forms of immorality?

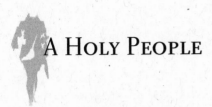

Chapter 4

A Holy People

"... and like living stones be yourselves built into a spiritual house, to be a holy priesthood...."

1 Peter 2:1-10

D r. Karl Menninger once observed that sin dropped out of the national vocabulary in the middle of the twentieth century.[1] The word no longer has a place in public discourse because it conveys images that the majority of the people will not accept. The word is still used in church, but it is no longer used in public debate by the nation's leaders and opinion-makers. Perhaps it was at the same time that another biblical word dropped out of the church's vocabulary. The words "holy" and "holiness," along with related words like "saint," have almost disappeared from the vocabulary of the church. When the words are used, they are not likely to be used with a favorable connotation.

These words have probably dropped from our vocabulary because they are filled with the negative associations that our culture has placed on them. "Holiness" brings to mind expressions like "holier than thou" or "holy Joe." The comedian refers

43

to the "weird holy man." In this context, what could be worse than to be called holy? It conjures up images of hermits, of religious people who live in isolation from the rest of the world. Someone once commented that the language of discipleship has been turned over to fanatics who do not fit into "mainstream" Christianity. In the same way, holiness has dropped out of the vocabulary of Christians.

The word is deeply rooted in both Old and New Testaments. It is used to describe the incomparable God who, in Miriam's song (Exod. 15:11), is "majestic in holiness, terrible in glorious deeds, doing wonders." As the one who is absolutely unique among the deities of the ancient world, God is holy. The holy God calls into being a "holy people," whose holiness rests on their encounter with Him. "For you are a people holy to the Lord your God," they are told in Deuteronomy 7:6. They are holy because "the Lord your God has chosen you to be a people for his own possession, out of all of the peoples that are on the face of the earth." They are a "kingdom of priests and a holy nation" (Exod. 19:6). As a holy people, they are set apart for God and set apart from the world. Consequently, their ethical behavior distinguishes them from the nations around them. The meaning of holiness is especially indicated in the moral imperatives that are given in the holiness code of Leviticus 17-26. "You shall be holy, as I am holy," they are told (Lev. 19:2). Their holiness means that they have been called out of environment to be God's own possession and to reject the abhorrent morality of their neighbors.

Throughout Israel's history, the tension was present between her natural inclination toward assimilation with the other nations and her memory that she had been selected to be a holy people. From the period of the Judges to the time of Jesus, Israel struggled with the meaning of holiness and the temptation toward assimilating with the larger culture.

Perhaps holiness dropped out of our vocabulary because we are accustomed to a Christian civilization where our Christianity seldom demanded that we stand apart from our society. Worldliness, the opposite of holiness, has also dropped from our vocabulary. Where we have made peace with our culture, the words "holiness" and "worldliness" lose their meaning, for we cannot imagine how Christianity would demand that we separate from the dominant standards of our own time.

Holiness disappeared from the vocabulary of Christians when they made peace with society. By the end of the twentieth century, the peace had been disturbed, and we no longer live in a Christian society. Thus our situation resembles the one of Christians in 1 Peter. Peter's call to his community was a reminder that their status as "aliens" was not an unfortunate accident, for God called Christians to "be holy as God is holy" (1 Pet. 1:15). Just as the ancient Israelites were summoned out from among their neighbors to be separate *for* God and *from* the society, the Christians who first read 1 Peter were challenged to "be holy." This challenge can especially be heard by Christians who live in a culture that has no respect for Christian traditions and morality.

The pressures to fit in were enormous for the first generation of Christians. New Christians—"newborn babes"—were faced with the challenge of "putting away" such elements of the old life as "malice and all guile and insincerity and envy and all slander" (2:1). The new birth, they learned, required the putting away of old habits as certainly as one puts away old clothes. It was this process of "putting away" that made them aliens in their own land and produced rejection and hostility in the populace (cf. 2:12).

How can one go about the business of being holy in the midst of enormous pressures to fit in? Sociologists remind us that those who hold the minority view are under extraordinary pressure to give up their "strange ideas." One who holds strange ideas is likely to be filled with self-doubt and insecurity. The pressure grows to accept the ideas that *everyone* knows to be true. Christians in the first century felt this pressure powerfully—and Christians today feel it too.

How do Christians meet the challenge, the social pressure, and the self-doubt that comes with holding minority views? One answer, of course, is to revise our Christianity until it offends no one. Another answer is provided by 1 Peter.

Come to Christ

1 Peter 2:4 offers an invitation to alien Christians to "Come to him, to that living stone." This new birth involves not only a "putting away" (2:1); it involves also "coming to" Jesus.

When we recall that the readers have already "come to" Jesus, we might be surprised at the invitation to Christians who are feeling the pressures of living as aliens. Apparently the Christian existence requires more than a once-for-all response to the invitation, for one continually comes to the "living stone."

What is most important about the living stone, according to First Peter, is that he was "rejected by men but in God's sight chosen and precious" (cf. Ps. 118:22; 1 Pet. 2:7). He was also the "stone of stumbling" mentioned in Isaiah (8:17). We are reminded of Paul's word to the Corinthians that "we preach Christ crucified, a stumbling block to Jews and folly to Gentiles" (1 Cor. 1:23). The cross was the constant reminder that Jesus was the outsider and alien. Christians are not invited simply to "come to Jesus," but to "stand on the side" of Jesus, the rejected one.

The little group of Christians, surrounded by a hostile environment, is to recognize that its distance from its culture is not an unfortunate circumstance. Christianity began with the "rejected one," and it is to the rejected Jesus— the one who died on a cross between two thieves—that they are invited to come.

In our culture, the invitation to "come to Jesus" has been heard in countless ways, and Jesus still remains a popular figure. Indeed, according to the Gallup polls, Jesus remains popular throughout the American populace. For some, he is the epitome of the well-adjusted figure and success story. It is easy to be attracted to this kind of figure. However, in 1 Peter we are reminded that Jesus did not "fit in." The cross is the reminder that Jesus was an outsider. When we come to Jesus, we stand on the side of the one who was an outsider in his own culture.

From the viewpoint of his own culture, Jesus was an outsider. There was, however, another side. The one who was "rejected by men" was "chosen and precious" in God's sight. The stone which the builders rejected has become "the head of the corner." God's judgments are not our judgments. What was absurd in human eyes was precious in God's sight. The "stone of stumbling" was in fact a "cornerstone, chosen and precious" (1 Pet. 2:6). Others may reject that stone (2:7), but Christians have chosen to live by the story of the one who was "chosen and precious."

A Spiritual House

The second resource for living in a hostile environment appears when we accept the invitation to come to Jesus. We who come to the "living stone" are in fact challenged to "be built into a spiritual house" and "to be a holy priesthood." Indeed, those who come to Jesus are, in fact, the "living stones" out of which the spiritual house is made. No one is asked to be an outsider alone, and no one is to be holy in isolation. We are reminded of Paul's doctrine of the church as the body of Christ. Whereas Paul describes members as the arms and legs, feet and hands, of Christ, 1 Peter describes "living stones" that are built into a house. New Christians are reminded that the growth process does not take place apart from the life of the community. Each of these "living stones" contributes to the building of the community, for everyone has received a gift that is to be employed for the benefit of the church (cf. 1 Pet. 4:10-11).

We are, of course, social beings, and we cannot imagine life that is not lived in community.

What life have you if you have not life together?
There is no life that is not in community,

wrote T. S. Eliot. Undoubtedly the Christians of Asia Minor could have chosen between a variety of communities to which they might have belonged. America, too, has countless opportunities for community life. Some communities are based on common interests, others are based on shared leisure-time activities, and others are based on professional life. First Peter refers to a different kind of community: a "holy priesthood."

Holiness was a good word for describing the community. Just as ancient Israel was to be a "kingdom of priests and a holy people" (Exod. 19:6), set apart from the nations around her to serve God, the Christian community is a holy people founded on the living stone that was rejected by men. In the cities where the Christians live, others will look at their strangeness and wonder why they reject the ways that have been "inherited from the fathers" (1:18). The Christians will be the objects of slander (2:12) and amazement

(4:4). At the work place and in the neighborhood they will be asked, often in a condescending manner, to explain why they follow such strange ways (3:15). Their answer is that they are a holy people, and they have built their lives on the rejected one.

The Qumran community, who left us the Dead Sea Scrolls, also saw themselves as the "holy people"; for this reason they retreated to the desert to live holy lives that were not tainted by the world around them. What the Christians of 1 Peter are asked to do may be more difficult. At the work place and in their villages, they are challenged to be a holy people and retain their separate identity when they are surrounded by the old ways. The pressures to conform are enormous. They probably experience economic disadvantages and social shame for their new moral standards. The community is the one place where they can be reminded that the outsiders are in fact the "holy people" who are precious to God. In church, their moral commitments are reinforced. They work out those commitments together, knowing that there are others who are not participating in the "drunkenness, revels, carousing, and lawless idolatry" of their neighbors (4:4). Their teachers hold before them the ideal of God's holy people from the past and encourage them to stay on the side of Jesus, the rejected one. In the fact that together they are a "holy priesthood," they find the resources to continue their exile existence.

Our situation in the twenty-first century is not very different from that of 1 Peter, for anyone who takes Christian commitments and Christian morality seriously will be placed in an uncomfortable position. The profession of Christianity in general may not block the promotion or stand in the way of one's popularity, but to take one's Christianity seriously is a different matter. A non-Christian culture, like that of 1 Peter, will be "surprised that you do not join them" (4:4) in ways that are contrary to the Christian faith. The one great resource for living the Christian life is to be found in the church as a "holy people."

As a people who live our Christian lives in the school and the marketplace, the consciousness of the church as a holy people is indispensable to maintaining our Christian identity and our values, for we are constantly bombarded by the other messages that are creating values. These values are antagonistic to the Christian faith. One of the major assumptions of our time, for example, is that we create our own ideas of right and wrong, and that each of us exists to exercise his or her freedom for self-fulfillment. The constant barrage of the media would convince us that we simply choose our own lifestyles, as if moral commitments were *matters of style.*

Several years ago, Nicholas Kristof, columnist for the *New York Times*, acknowledged that he disagreed with Evangelical Christians on almost every issue, but added, "Nearly all of us in the news business are completely out of touch with a group that includes 46 percent of Americans."[2] "Losing their Religion" was the title of a recent *Newsweek* article in which the author observed the total absence of religious themes in television drama.[3] Responding to the *New York Times'* wholehearted support for abortion rights, a writer in the *New York Times Magazine* wrote that "it is a shared, if unspoken premise of the world that most of us inhabit that absolutes do not exist and that people who claim them are crazy."[4] One writer has suggested that television now forms the value in our civilization and is the most ubiquitous teacher that any civilization ever had—running for an average of seven and a half hours a day in ninety-eight percent of American homes.[5]

How does the church maintain its identity in a world where our culture's greatest teacher is the media? I suggest that we have reached a very critical era when we must once more rediscover the idea of the church as a "holy people." In the midst of the pervasive influence of the mass culture, we come together regularly to be nourished by a different story. Under the guidance of good preachers and teachers, we come together to learn how to be a "holy people." We leave our services encouraged to say "no" to the messages of our culture and reminded that Jesus was the outsider who led a counterculture.

In a university class that I taught for many semesters on the subject of marriage and family, I frequently asked university students from a variety of religious traditions to tell me what they had been taught in their own heritage about the subject of divorce. I expected to hear views reflecting the centuries of debate on the subject they had been transmitted in local congregations; but to my surprise few students had any idea what was expected of them. The experience reinforced for me the fact that a major function of Christian teaching is instruction on how to be a holy people. The early Christian epistles, which were read in church, were filled with concrete instructions on the Christian life: lists of vices to "put off" and positive attributes to "put on." Christians were taught that they belonged to a moral community, and Christians met to reinforce moral qualities in each other.

In *What's Right with the Church*, William Willimon has reminded us that our actions flow from our identity. "We learn our ethics as we learn language, as incidental to growing up with certain people, not because someone sat us down and taught us." In the church, he says, we learn who we are, our moral possibilities are broadened, "and our present actions are placed in a larger context than what merely seems right to us in the moment."[6]

If we are to be a "holy people" in a secular culture, we must begin by reintroducing the concept of holiness to a church that has forgotten the word itself. The Christian message will not be a warmed-over version of those things that play well in the media. Our worship services will remind us that we have our own story of the one who said "no" to the messages of self-gratification, the lust for power, and the desire for pleasure. He formed a community which sought to pattern its life after that story. In church we recall that Jesus was the rejected one, but that the rejected one was in fact "chosen and precious" in the sight of God. In realizing that we are his holy people, we are equipped to behave as holy people.

NOTES

1   James H. Billington, "Education and Culture: Beyond Lifestyles," in Richard John Neuhaus, ed., *Virtue—Public and Private* (Grand Rapids:

2   Nicholas Kristof, "God, Satan and the Media," *New York Times*, March 4, 2003. http://bobby2.wordpress.com/2003/god-satan-and-the-media.

3   *Newsweek* 27 July 2009, at http://www.newsweek.com/id/207059.2009

4   *New York Times Magazine*, March 1999.

5   Billington, "Education and Culture," 3.

6   William Willimon, *What's Right with the Church?* (San Francisco: Harper & Row, 1985), 82.

Questions for Discussion

1. According to 1 Peter, what specific kinds of behavior were Christians to abandon in order to be holy? What differences in lifestyle distinguish Christians from other good moral people?

2. In your own experience, to what extent are the commonly accepted values socially determined? If one who holds different views is likely to be intimidated, what means are available for Christians to resist the pressure of conformity?

3. According to 1 Peter 2:4-10, what are the two major resources that allow Christians to live in a hostile environment?

4. To what extent is Jesus commonly understood as the "rejected" or "unpopular" one? Is Jesus more popular than Christianity?

5. How is the holy life of Christians different from that of other groups that have tried to be a holy people, including the Qumran community?

6. Discuss the ways in which television is our society's teacher. What can a "holy people" do to counteract this influence?

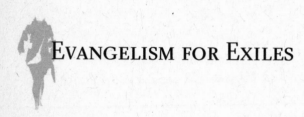

Chapter 5

EVANGELISM FOR EXILES

"... that you may declare the wonderful deeds of him who called you out of darkness into his marvelous light."
1 Peter 2:9-12

Leslie Newbigin served nearly forty years as a missionary in India before he returned to England to teach and to be a missionary in an inner-city area. His return to his native land and his observation of the religious conditions there provoked him to ask the question: "What would be involved in a genuinely missionary encounter between the gospel and ... 'modern Western culture'?"[1] After spending the major part of his life as a missionary in the Far East, he recognized that his native England presented a major challenge to the proclamation of the gospel.

In very important ways, the task of evangelism is a greater challenge in the Western world than in the Third World. Dr. Newbigin says, "In great areas of Asia, Africa, and Oceania, the church grows steadily and even spectacularly. But in the areas dominated by modern Western culture (whether in its capitalist or socialist political expressions), the church is shrinking and the gospel falls on deaf ears."[2] Our own experience confirms Dr. Newbigin's assessment. We hear of the vitality of the faith in distant places under the worst conditions imaginable. Civil wars, government oppression, and economic disaster cannot stop the growth of Christianity in some parts of the Third World. In our own country, however, we have watched as congregations have grown older and smaller. We have also seen frustration and uncertainty about the entire evangelistic task.

Evangelism is a problem for us, in the first place, because the word suggests methods and a mentality from the past that make us uncomfortable. The mentality suggested the arrogance of one who had all of the answers, and this view made us uncomfortable. The methods borrowed from principles of salesmanship also disillusioned us with evangelism. A colleague tells me that the textbook used for a college course in personal evangelism was Dale Carnegie's *How to Win Friends and Influence People*. The suggestion was, of course, that evangelism consists mainly in learning principles of salesmanship, even manipulation. For many of us, this approach to evangelism was shallow enough to give the idea a bad name.

Evangelism is also a problem because we face a country that has heard the message before. It has been heard in church and on television and radio. We have the impression that the public has become saturated with the Christian message. Undoubtedly one of the most difficult tasks of all is to speak the Christian message to those who have already heard it.

How does the church present the good news to a culture that seems to be inoculated against it? One of the most frequent responses in recent years has been the attempt to clothe the message in language that is more acceptable to the contemporary audience.

This approach, of course, has much to commend it, for we discover already in the New Testament that the message is presented in terms that can be understood by the listeners. Paul's speech at Athens (Acts 17:22-31) is very different from his evangelistic messages to Jewish audiences (cf. Acts 13:16-41). Nevertheless, Paul did not simply adapt his message to fit the tastes of his audience. In each case, the central Christian convictions about Jesus and the resurrection were unmistakably present.

James Hunter, in *American Evangelicalism*, has pointed out that an extraordinary amount of contemporary evangelical literature consists of accommodating the Christian message to the prevailing tastes of the time. Hunter observes the book titles that come from evangelical publishing houses, and notes that Christianity is commended in this literature in ways that reflect a new attempt to accommodate to the questions that are presently being asked. Only recently, he says, "has literature been published with such titles as *God's Psychiatry* (Allen, 1953), *The Sensation of Being Somebody: Building an Adequate Self-Concept* (Wagner, 1979), *The Art of Getting Along with People* (Osborne, 1979), reflecting a unique subjectivism in the Evangelical worldview."[3] Other popular books include *God's Key to Health and Happiness* (1976), *The Art of Understanding Yourself* (1968), and *Do I Have to Be Me?* (Ahlem, 1973).[4] While many of the questions are legitimate ones, the central theme running through this literature consists of demonstrating that Christianity appeals to our drive for self-actualization, happiness, and personal fulfillment. Christianity is packaged and marketed in such a way that it appeals to the selfishness and individual drive for personal pleasure that dominates our culture. Hunter says, "An important consequence of Evangelicalism's accommodation to modernity has been its increased marketability in a highly competitive religious marketplace."[5] Features of Christianity that might be found objectionable are minimized or ignored because of the demands of "marketing the product."

A contemporary approach to evangelism and church growth is to offer a Christianity that maximizes the benefits of Christianity to the consumer. Christianity is marketed as the key to successful family life or the source of proper self-esteem. While it may be true that the Christian life does produce better marriages, better self-esteem, and greater personal happiness, another side of the Christian life is often ignored. As we recall from 1 Peter, the joy of the Christian faith may indeed be associated with having a message that makes one a stranger in his own land. The personal happiness of Christians in the first century was not that of American self-indulgence, but the joy of sharing in the sufferings of Christ.

The Christianity that grows by careful market analysis and by careful attention to "what the consumers are buying" will lose its identity. Under these conditions it may grow when it has little left to say.

Evangelism for Aliens

The question sometimes raised by classical scholars is, "Why did Christianity win?" How did this movement spread under such unbearable conditions? They did not win through market analysis, for the Christians were the objects of ridicule and slander. Indeed, the hostility apparent in 1 Peter results from the fact that they have separated themselves from the "traditions of the fathers" (1:18) and maintained their identity so strongly that they were persecuted. It was as if they had built walls around themselves to separate from their own culture. A "holy people" needed the walls that separated them from the practices of their neighbors (cf. 4:4).

For some who choose to be a holy people, evangelism is impossible. The Qumran community, with its conviction about the corruption of society, was scarcely evangelistic, for it placed the holiness of the community above outreach. Throughout the history of Christianity, one of the options of those who wished to maintain their holiness was to separate from the evils of the world. This option, however, is not the one recommended in 1 Peter. The task of the "holy people," according to 1 Peter 2:9, was to "declare the wonderful deeds of him who called you out of darkness into his marvelous light" (2:9). Even in a hostile climate, the church has an evangelistic task.

The Christians of 1 Peter were not intimidated by their role as "aliens and exiles." Nor did they echo the dominant voices in their culture. Like the Israelites in Isaiah 42:12 who were challenged to "declare his praise in the coastlands," the Christians are to "declare" what God has done. The word "declare" (*exangello*), used in 1 Peter with the purpose clause ("that you may declare") reminds us that the Christian community faces the world with full confidence in its message. The Christian community is not to be forever listening to the voices of culture in order for its voice to harmonize with prevailing tastes. Instead, it confidently *declares* its message.

The evangelistic message grows out of the conviction that God has "called us out of darkness into his marvelous light" (1 Pet. 2:9). We are reminded of Jesus' statement to his disciples: "You are the light of the world. A city set on a hill cannot be hid" (Matt. 5:14-16).

At the end of the first century, evangelism took place under conditions that would seem intolerable to us. The entire book of 1 Peter suggests the hostility and suspicion with which the pagan neighbors looked at the Christians. In that society, evangelistic programs, door-knocking campaigns, and other means to gain visibility were unthinkable. Nevertheless the movement grew enough that the pagan neighbors were increasingly bothered by its expansion. It is often asked how Christianity triumphed and drove the competition from the field under these unfavorable conditions. Nothing was more powerful for these Christians than the conviction that they had found the light, a message they declared wherever they went.

Sometimes this word was declared to the pagans who visited Christian assemblies. In 1 Corinthians 14:23 Paul is conscious of the impact of the Christian assembly on outsiders. The original readers of 1 Peter are reminded that they were "born anew . . . through the living and abiding word of God" (1:23). They are told that "that word is the good news which was preached to you" (1:25). Perhaps many of the readers themselves had first been converted through the power of the preaching that they heard in Christian assemblies. The clear, forceful message made an impression on them which they could not forget.

At other times the word was declared by the individual Christians who took the message to the neighborhood and the workplace. We have no records of organized evangelistic work in the ancient church, and yet the church grew remarkably in some areas. Celsus, one ancient pagan writer, complained that Christians aggressively proclaimed their faith in homes and at the workplace. This conviction that they had been "called out of darkness into his marvelous light" mobilized Christians in their private lives, and it gave power to Christian assemblies where the word of God was preached with passion and conviction.

Is evangelism possible in a culture that has turned committed Christians into "aliens and exiles?" The epistle of 1 Peter is a reminder that evangelism can take place in the worst of times *when Christians are convinced that they have been called out of darkness into his marvelous light.* I am convinced that what we need in order to have an effective evangelistic witness is not a message that has been trimmed to fit prevailing tastes. Evangelism does not grow out of our gaining a greater command of mass media, marketing technique, or the means of persuasion.

Why has evangelism fallen out of favor? Perhaps it has fallen out of favor because we are not certain what to say. In the absence of something to say, we spend our time echoing what others have already said.

An Evangelistic Lifestyle

In the new section of 1 Peter, which begins at 2:11 and extends through chapter three, we discover that the power of early Christianity was not limited to the spoken word. The section concerns Christian moral behavior, and it includes specific advice on how to live in a pagan society. Advice is given on the Christian's relationship to government, on the Christian slave's attitude to his pagan master, and on the Christian wife's attitude to her husband (2:13-3:7). Behind the advice, apparently, was a recognition that pagans noticed the conduct of the Christians. Indeed, Christians are reminded that "[the Gentiles] speak evil of you as wrongdoers" (2:12). Undoubtedly the separation of Christians from others and their strange ways (cf. 4:3-4) caused rumors to spread among the pagan neighbors.

The moral advice that is given in the new section begins with a reminder that Christians are to "abstain from the passions of the flesh that wage war against the soul" (2:11). Abstinence from these passions (*epithumiai*) was to be the identifying sign of the Christian community in a world enslaved to its own lusts. A community not enslaved to its passions was different in that society. Already in the epistle we have been reminded that slavery to these "passions" belongs to the old lifestyle (cf. 1:14, "your former passions"; cf. 4:3).

The word for "passions" (*epithumiai*), which refers to sexual passions, literally refers to any *desire* or *longing*. It can sometimes be used for desires that are proper. But it is most commonly used for improper selfish desires. The challenge to Christians in 2:11 is to abstain from every desire for self-fulfillment that does not include submission to God.

The reason for this advice is that Christian conduct is noticed by others. Although Christians are "aliens and exiles," they have not built walls of separation around them, for they "maintain good conduct among the Gentiles" (2:12). They demonstrate among their neighbors a life that is not enslaved to their own desire for self-realization.

The result of "maintaining good conduct among the Gentiles" is that Christians have an evangelistic impact on their neighbors. "They may see your good deeds and glorify God on the day of visitation." That is, the Christian lifestyle is noticed! Evangelism takes place not only with the proclamation of the word, but in the neighborhoods and at the workplaces where people notice the transformation that has taken place in Christian lives.

The evangelistic impact of Christian lives is one of the threads that runs through the epistle of 1 Peter. Christian wives may win their pagan husbands to the faith "without a word" (3:1). Pagan critics are silenced, not by Christian arguments, but by Christian lives (2:15). The evangelistic strategy of 1 Peter included the power of dedicated lives to win over those who first scorned the strangeness of the alien lifestyle.

Throughout the early church, nothing was more effective in evangelism than Christian communities that were noticeably different from their pagan surroundings. Christians consistently appealed to each other to live in such a way that their neighbors could see the difference Christ had made. We are reminded of Jesus' challenge to the disciples to be a "city set on a hill which cannot be hid." He knew that the result would be that "men will see your good works and glorify your father in heaven" (Matt. 5:16). Paul says of the Philippians that they "shine as lights in the world" (2:15). He advises the Colossians, "Conduct yourselves wisely toward outsiders" (Col. 4:5). To the Thessalonians he writes, "so that you may command the respect of outsiders" (4:12).

Did the strategy work? Historians list as one of the chief reasons for the triumph of Christianity the fact that Christians made high moral demands and had the power to live up to these demands. A clear alternative was offered to the decadent pagan society, and many chose the stern discipline of the Christian community over the paganism that demanded nothing.

What is the key to effective evangelism in an increasingly non-Christian culture? What could be more powerful and more compelling than communities which present an alternative lifestyle or counterculture to the prevailing norms? Imagine a community that is shaped by the gospel message of selflessness, a community where ambition, pride, and the hunger for power have no place. A community that finds joy in single-minded commitment to the faith would be powerful enough to win over many of the most cynical critics of Christianity, for no one could argue against the power of Christian lives.

I read recently of a missionary in India who went from village to village entertaining the people with films and magic tricks before he spoke to them about Christ. Once when he spoke of Christ, an elderly man, a Hindu, stood up and said:

Dear pastor, we have listened with interest, yes, with respect, to your words about Jesus Christ. We love Christ
and honor him as a unique man and as God. We also
like to read the Bible, when we have the time and are not
too tired. But, pardon me for saying this, this does not
make us want to become Christians. Don't we know your
parishioners? Don't we know how they live? How much
hostility and enmity, how much drunkenness and deceit
there is among them? They live no better than we do.[6]

NOTES

1 Leslie Newbigin, *Foolishness to the Greeks* (Grand Rapids: Eerdmans, 1986), 1.
2 Ibid., 3.
3 James Hunter, *American Evangelicalism: Conservative Religion and the Quandary of Modernity* (New Brunswick, N.J.: Rutgers University Press, 1983), 93-94.
4 Ibid., 95.
5 Ibid., 99.
6 Gerhard Lohfink, *Jesus and Community* (Philadelphia: Fortress, 1984), 146.

Questions for Discussion

1. Describe the changes you have observed in the place of evangelism in the life of the church. How do you account for the changes?

2. To what event should evangelists adapt their message to the audience? What are the advantages? What are the dangers?

3. According to historians, why did Christianity win?

4. What opportunities did the early church have for evangelism?
Compare them with the kinds of opportunities the church
has today.

5. What is an evangelistic lifestyle? Is the evangelistic lifestyle
described in 1 Peter likely to be effective?

6. Compare evangelism with salesmanship. To what extent are
the techniques of salesmanship appropriate for evangelism?

7. If one looks at the evangelical book market, what are the most
common approaches today to evangelism?

Chapter 6

FREEDOM FOR EXILES

"Live as free men, yet without using your freedom as a pretext for evil; but live as servants of God."

1 Peter 2:13-17

In one of the most significant books of the 1980s, Robert Bellah and a team of sociologists wrote *Habits of the Heart: Individualism and Commitment in American Life*. It is a study of the American character—"our habits of the heart" and our deeply held values. One of the most treasured of all values is that of freedom. The authors say, "Freedom is perhaps the most resonant, deeply held American value. In some ways, it defines the good in both personal and political life."[1]

Our most cherished national documents remind us of the place of freedom in our national consciousness. Many of us memorized long ago the words of the Declaration of Independence: "We hold these truths to be self-evident that all men are created equal, and that they are endowed by their Creator with certain unalienable rights." We also learned Lincoln's words, "Our forefathers brought forth on this continent a new nation, conceived in liberty and dedicated to the proposition that all men are created equal." We may be a nation of many different traditions, but the language of freedom has been the one value that was shared by all.

In our own generation we have witnessed breathtaking changes in the extension of human rights, as successive groups appealed to our founding documents to assert their rights to equality under the law. Rights that were originally extended only to white males have been expanded to include women and the descendants of black slaves. Basic rights have also been extended to the elderly. We continue to debate questions about the rights of children. In some instances, the process of extending these rights has been painful and divisive. The debate continues today, and each time the debate is based on an appeal to our deeply held love of freedom.

Freedom in Our Culture

While we may all appeal to the idea of freedom, we are less certain what it means to be free. The authors of *Habits of the Heart* conclude that:

> ... freedom turns out to mean being left alone by others, not having other people's values, ideas, or styles of life forced upon one, being free of arbitrary authority in work, family, and political life. What it is that one might do with his freedom is much more difficult for Americans to define. And if the entire social world is made up of individuals, each endowed with the right to be free of others' demands, it becomes hard to forge bonds of attachment, or cooperation with other people, since such bonds would imply obligations that necessarily impinge on one's freedom.[2]

The freedom that we cherish in our own culture is the freedom of individuals to assert themselves. Individual freedom thus takes its place before the interests of the group. In this kind of culture, government, marriage, and other relationships serve primarily the interests of individuals. Our society is a collection of interest groups, each one intent on asserting its own rights. Because institutions exist only to enhance the self-fulfillment of individuals, they are frequently cast aside when they seem to inhibit our freedom.

Christian Freedom

If freedom is a highly treasured value in our own society, it is also an important word for the church. "Live as free men," the recipients of 1 Peter are told (2:16). Their freedom is described as the condition of those who were "ransomed from the futile ways inherited from your fathers" (1:18). The new existence meant freedom from the bondage of the past.

The love of freedom is found throughout the New Testament, and especially in Paul's letters. "Where the Spirit of the Lord is, there is freedom," Paul says (2 Cor. 3:17). "For freedom Christ has set us free," he exclaims to the Galatians (5:1; cf. 5:13). Paul affirms his own freedom (1 Cor. 9:1), and he is determined that no one will subject him again to bondage (Gal. 2:4). The new existence in Christ means freedom from the bondage to the law (Rom. 7:3; 8:2). Christians are not slaves, but enjoy the freedom of adult children in their father's house (cf. Gal. 4:1-6).

Freedom is, of course, a precious word in every culture. It is the rallying cry for oppressed peoples around the world. It seems to be the most treasured word for revolutionaries who rally the people to throw off a colonial power. It is the favorite word for oppressed minorities who want to claim their basic dignity in their own country. Even well-fed, upwardly mobile citizens of western countries still demand freedoms that they believe are denied them. Because freedom is the favorite word of such diverse groups, one suspects that the word means different things to different people.

A Misunderstood Word

Perhaps it was because freedom could have many different meanings that the early Christian writers scarcely use the word without warning against a misunderstanding (cf. 1 Cor. 6:12; 10:23; Gal. 5:1, 13). The same concern is apparent in the advice given in 1 Peter 2:16, "Live as free men, yet without using your freedom as a pretext for evil; but live as servants of God." There was the danger that Christians might confuse their Christian freedom with all of the associations that word had in their pagan environment. Under these circumstances, freedom could be turned into a noble-sounding pretext to cover what Christians might want to do for their own selfish motives.

For 1 Peter, freedom meant, in the first place, being "ransomed from the traditions of the fathers" (1:18). One can imagine the questions that faced new Christians who asked what it meant to be liberated from these old traditions. They could have concluded that the new alien lifestyle involved freedom from the obligations to the society which looked on them with disdain. New questions continually faced them: Were they free from their old obligations to their government, their fellow-citizens, their superiors, their parents, their families? Did freedom now mean that they could withdraw from these old obligations to pursue their own private interests? The Christian slaves wondered if their new freedom released them from the institution of slavery, with all of its cruelty.

Christian wives must have asked if they now were expected to show respect for their pagan husbands.

Rumors were circulating about the Christians. Ancient writers regarded them in the same way that we might regard the members of a strange new cult. Indeed, Christians were considered dangerous because they broke with traditions that were firmly held. Tacitus, the Roman historian, said of the Jews, "And the earliest lesson they receive is to despise the gods, to disown their country, and to regard their parents, children, and brothers as of little account."[3] The same charges could have been made against Christians. They were considered dangerous to the established institutions.

Christians were indeed vulnerable in this society, for they appeared to undermine established traditions. According to 1 Peter 4:4, they apparently refused to participate in the festivals of the community. One can imagine what these little enclaves of Christians meant to the families left behind.

How were the Christians to live out their freedom from the "traditions of the fathers?" One can imagine the slanders from neighbors, husbands, masters, and magistrates (cf. 2:12; 3:16). What did it mean to live as aliens and exiles? Were they free from these institutions where they were being slandered? Were slaves and women to assert their freedom from the established institutions of slavery and marriage, particularly when they were associated with non-Christians? Were they free from the government which did not respect their rights?

Although our questions are not precisely those that were being asked in 1 Peter, we too struggle with the meaning of Christian freedom. Like the Christians of the first century, we have difficulty speaking of freedom apart from the associations the word has in our culture. Our temptation is to speak of Christian freedom as if it meant asserting one's own rights, being left alone by others, fulfilling our own potential. I recall an article that appeared some years ago in *The Christian Century*, challenging us to rethink the traditional Christian prohibition of divorce. The author said: "If Jesus allowed for breaking the honored Sabbath laws. . . , would he now allow for a suspension of the proscription against divorce if such were to liberate a person from the bondage to an intolerable marriage? . . . does it now follow that marriage was made for humanity, rather than humanity for marriage? If the institution, important as it is, does violence to the individual, then shouldn't the institution be amended in order that the individual might fluourish?"[4]

The freedom the author advocated was merely the freedom of our contemporary culture, the freedom of self-fulfillment, wrapped in a Christian veneer.

How is Christian freedom to be distinguished from the freedom which our culture cherishes? In 1 Peter 2:11 a new section begins, which extends to 4:11. The subject of this new section is the conduct of Christians in their normal relationships. Although Christians are addressed as "aliens and exiles," they do not retreat from the world around them, for they maintain "good conduct among the Gentiles" (2:12). The following sections address the many ways in which Christians maintain this good conduct among the Gentiles, for Christians are addressed as citizens, slaves, wives, and husbands who interact daily with the non-Christian world. Unlike the Qumran community, which had retreated to the desert to maintain its holiness, the Christian exiles remained within the institutions of society where their behavior was noticed. Although they had been "ransomed from the traditions of the fathers" (1:18), their freedom did not release them from their place in society.

A remarkable fact about this alien existence is that Christians are challenged to "maintain good conduct among the Gentiles, so that in case they speak of you as wrongdoers, they may see your good works and glorify God on the day of visitation" (2:12). Rumors were spreading that Christians were so unconcerned about their world that they undermined society, but Christians were challenged to do good. Their good conduct would silence those who spread the rumor that Christians undermined society (cf. 2:15, 20; 3:1-2). Christians were expected to be good citizens, slaves, and wives within a non-Christian world. Freedom was no pretext for liberation from these institutions.

Perhaps the most remarkable fact about this alien existence is that it involved conduct that seemed to fit in with the cultural values of their own time. Christians were challenged to be "good" in a way that their pagan neighbors would appreciate their conduct. Indeed, the word rendered "do right" in the RSV (*agathopoiein*) appears three times in this section (2:15, 20; 3:6) to describe the Christian behavior that should impress their pagan neighbors. Apparently there were ways in which Christians and pagans shared the same moral concepts. For both Christians and pagans, there was a concept of "doing right," and Christian freedom did not release anyone from the obligation to "do right."

The Freedom of Submissiveness

The Christians of 1 Peter were not addressed in vague generalities about the proper conduct of aliens, for the section in 2:13-3:7 speaks specifically about the obligations of Christian freedom. Perhaps the most remarkable feature of this entire section is that in the three successive paragraphs Christians are addressed with the simple verb, "be subject" or "be submissive" (*hypotassein*). All Christians are charged to be submissive to governing authorities. Christian slaves are charged to be submissive to Christian masters; and Christian wives are challenged to be submissive to their non-Christian husbands. All of these commandments are given in the midst of instructions which assume the existence of Christian freedom. Christian freedom (2:16) is experienced in the midst of submission!

The verb *hypotassein* is derived from the Greek words *hypo* ("under") and *tassein* ("to order, institute, or place"), and it is related to the noun *taxis* ("order," cf. 1 Cor. 14:40, "decently and in order"). The focus of the word is on placing oneself in an orderly arrangement. *Hypotassein* involves living an orderly life by accepting one's place or one's position in life. The opposite of "submission" would be to seek one's own advantage or to resist one's circumstances (cf. Rom. 13:5).

This word stands at the center of early Christian moral instruction. When Paul instructs Christians on their relationship to the government, he uses forms of *hypotassein* and *tassein* repeatedly in Romans 13 (13:1, 2, 5). He uses the word for the relationship of Christians to each other (cf. 1 Cor. 16:16). In the passages on the household in Colossians 3:18 and Ephesians 5:21, he uses the word for the relationship of family members to each other. Thus for both Paul's letters and the epistle of 1 Peter, "submission" is a central word for Christian conduct (cf. also Tit. 2:5; 3:1). The word characterizes the Christians in their preference for order and their determination not to seek first their own interests.

The emphasis on submission is especially remarkable in a book written to "aliens and exiles," for the advice to "submit" appears to be a call to "adapt" or "accommodate" Christian conduct to the prevailing moral climate. Ancient writers agreed with the teaching of 1 Peter that everyone should submit to the government; that slaves should submit to their masters; that wives should be submissive to their husbands. The advice that is given in 1 Peter 2:13-3:7 seems, on the surface, to be identical with the morality of that time and scarcely the strange morality of "aliens and exiles."

What is the morality of aliens and exiles? We have seen, in the first place, that in many instances the Christians were known for their strange conduct (cf. 4:4, "They are surprised that you do not now join them. . . ."). Yet Christian moral teaching sometimes agreed with that of the pagan neighbors. Yet even where Christian morality seemed to fit in with its culture, it was different nonetheless, for Christian morality had a new motivation.

It was not only for the sake of fitting in to the morality of the day that the readers of this letter are challenged to "submit to every human institution" (cf. 2:13). Indeed, Christians could show that they were not conformed to the world in their acts of submission to others, for their submission was at the heart of their faith. Submission, like humility, was a word that took on a new dignity among Christians. Those who have the superior social position are reminded not to be domineering toward those whose position is inferior (3:7; cf. 5:3), and those who are placed in an inferior position are challenged to "be subject" (cf. 5:5). All Christians are called upon to clothe themselves with humility toward each other, "for God opposes the proud, but gives grace to the humble" (5:5). The entire community is instructed to "have unity of spirit, sympathy, love of the brethren, a tender heart and a humble mind" (3:8). They are to practice nonresistance, and to resist the temptation to return evil for evil (3:9). Submission, therefore, belongs to a broader context of early Christian morality.

Christians knew the story of Christ, the submissive one, and that story shaped their attitude toward the society around them. When the whole community learned that story, together they shared the new value that was given to humility.

Submission Today

The advice in 1 Peter was expressed in an ancient society where the rule of the Roman emperor and his local governors (2:13) was supreme. Christians were taught not to despise the rule of law nor to challenge its authority, but to demonstrate their willingness to serve the greater good of society by contributing to public order. Despite the charges made against them, they would demonstrate Christian humility in their lives as citizens. Christian exiles joined their neighbors in their respect for an orderly life.

In *Habits of the Heart*, the authors observe that, while Americans treasure their freedom to have a part in shaping the destiny of their country, they also see their freedom largely in terms of their own narrow political interests. Indeed, our freedom consists largely in the rights of interest groups who demand their rights, even at the expense of the larger body. To play partisan politics is to seek the advantage of one's own group. To rise "above politics" is to seek the public good.[5]

The instruction of 1 Peter is for Christians to live as good citizens, preferring the welfare of the entire society over their own well-being. In a society where groups demand their own rights, Christians are known for the submission that looks to the interest of others. Those who practice Christian submission will be exiles in their own land, and they will present a new idea of freedom to their society. This new kind of freedom will have a positive impact on those who observe the selflessness of Christians (2:15; cf. 2:12).

NOTES

1   Robert Bellah, et al, *Habits of the Heart* (Berkeley: University of California Press, 1985), 23.
2   Ibid.
3   Tacitus, History. V. 5.
4   Robert F. Sinks, "A Theology of Divorce," *Christian Century* 94 (1977): 378.
5   Bellah, *Habits of the Heart*, 202.

Questions for Discussion

1. What is the most common definition of freedom in our society? To what extent do popular conceptions strengthen or undermine the life of the larger communities?

2. Give examples of the fact that early Christians constantly were concerned about the misunderstanding of freedom.

3. In what ways were Christians considered dangerous to established institutions?

4. In what ways did Christian conduct fit in with the conduct of non-Christians? Does Christian conduct often fit in with society?

5. How does Christian freedom involve submission?

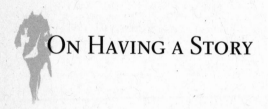

Chapter 7

ON HAVING A STORY

"For to this end you have been called, because Christ also suffered for you. . . ."

1 Peter 2:18-25

The biblical passages that refer to slavery have always been an embarrassment to enlightened Christians of modern times, for nothing offends our sense of decency more than the idea of holding another person in bondage. The passages present special difficulties for students of American history, for our nation was deeply scarred by the issue of slavery. The wounds of that terrible conflict remain a part of American life. Oppressors appealed to these passages for support in defending their oppression, arguing that Christianity stood on the side of power and against the weak and powerless. In some cases, the oppressed also concluded that Christianity stood on the side of the powerful who robbed them of their dignity.

Although the New Testament dignifies slaves by indicating that "there is neither slave nor free" (Gal. 3:28; cf. 1 Cor. 7:22), it does not challenge the institution itself. While slaves and masters came together in the church as brothers and sisters in Christ, slaves remained slaves. Undoubtedly the new relationship in Christ improved their situation, for masters are warned against abusing their slaves (Eph. 6:9; Col. 4:1). Nevertheless slavery is a fact in the New Testament, as it was in the Greco-Roman world.

Modern readers may have difficulty visualizing ancient slavery without reading into the text the ideas that come from the American experience, for ancient slavery was not based on color or the horror of the slave trade of more recent times. In ancient times, one could be a slave either from birth or from the misfortune of being captured in war. At times slaves had responsible positions in the household, and in many instances they were well educated. In some instances a slave could purchase his own freedom and then enter into public life. Epictetus, for example, who lived from A.D. 55 to 135, grew up as a slave before being set free. From there he became an important Stoic philosopher.

Although ancient slaves might be well educated and hold responsible positions, their experience contained much of the dehumanizing impact that accompanied slavery in the American experience. In both cases slaves were property, and they were dependent on the kindness of the masters. Some lived in tolerable circumstances, but others were the victims of sadistic masters. While some protection existed for slaves under Roman law, masters often tortured and even killed their slaves without fear of punishment.

As Christianity spread, slaves entered the church in great numbers. Sometimes entire households were converted at once (cf. Acts 16:15; 18:8; 1 Cor. 1:16). Apparently slaves were numbered in many of these households, for the members of Christian households are sometimes addressed (cf. Col. 3:18-4:1; Eph. 5:21-6:9).

In other instances slave owners apparently became Christians without their slaves, as in the case of Philemon. There were also instances where slaves became Christians apart from their masters. This was apparently the case in 1 Peter.

The advice to slaves in 1 Peter contains the reminder about the more tragic aspects of slavery. Although some slaves were fortunate enough to serve good and kind masters (cf. 2:18), others served under "overbearing" (RSV) or "harsh" (NIV) masters. The word for "overbearing" (*skolios*) means literally "crooked" or "perverse." Slaves had no rights in the presence of perverse, sadistic masters, and it was not uncommon for slaves to suffer unjustly at the whim of their masters. If the Christian community was vulnerable in the midst of a hostile society, Christian slaves were even more vulnerable. Even if Christianity had not threatened the institution of slavery itself, their pagan masters could never be absolutely certain of the loyalty of those slaves who belonged to a strange new religion. We can imagine the potential for conflict when Christian slaves insisted on going off to what appeared to be a secret meeting. Their Christian commitment could have been the source for their being singled out to become the objects of a special kind of discrimination. While the whole church was suffering the effects of discrimination, no one experienced it more than those who had no civil rights.

The slaves had undoubtedly heard that they, along with other Christians, were free in Christ (1 Pet. 2:16) and "ransomed from the traditions of the fathers" (1:18). Perhaps they wondered if this new freedom in Christ liberated them from an evil institution. Did their existence as Christian exiles allow them to rebel against harsh masters or at least to escape from this demeaning existence? Christian slaves might easily have concluded that they could serve

God more easily if only they had a better place to serve him. However, they are instructed to "be submissive to your masters with all respect." Not only are they to submit to the kind and gentle masters, but also to the overbearing, cruel masters, even if it meant suffering unjustly at the whim of these masters.

Why do the New Testament writings, including 1 Peter, not challenge the institution that destroyed all human dignity? In the first place, early Christians, meeting as small enclaves in the major cities with a large slave membership, had none of the resources for such a massive economic restructuring of society. In a civilization built largely on this institution, this task would have been unthinkable.

The advice in 1 Peter points to another important reason why the institution is mentioned without objection. *Submission* for Christians has taken on an entirely new meaning, for all Christians have learned the value of "counting others better than themselves" (cf. Phil. 2:3). Christians look to the interests of others, and not only to their own interests. Thus slaves are instructed to be submissive, not because Christianity is always on the side of the oppressors, but because submission lies at the heart of Christian behavior.

At first it appears that the morality of Christian slaves is the same as that which was expected of all slaves: to fit in with popular expectation, to accept their place. Is this morality different from the common morality of the culture? The new feature is that Christian slaves have discovered that their plight is not only something to endure. In suffering unjustly they can demonstrate the new value that Christianity places on submission under circumstances that are harsh and unfair. They can experience freedom even here.

Paradigms for the Church

If the advice to the exiles of the cities of Asia Minor seems far removed from the experience of modern urban Americans, advice to the slaves of those areas seems at first to be even more remote from our own experience. What can this advice possibly mean to those of us who cannot comprehend the discrimination and suffering of ancient household slaves? One commentator has suggested that the advice to slaves in 1 Peter is the heart of the letter, for what the slaves were experiencing—unjust suffering and discrimination—was what all Christian exiles were discovering in their relationship with the world around them. While slaves knew unjust suffering at its worst, the entire Christian community discovered that their Christian commitment involved suffering for their faith. Christianity had not brought peace and tranquility, but a time of testing (1:6-8) where they knew how to suffer as Christians (cf. 4:16). The Christian life was precarious for all of the Christian exiles.

When we discover that the words to slaves were in fact addressed to all Christians who suffer unjustly from discrimination, the instructions become more than an embarrassing acceptance of the status quo and a bit of favoritism for those in power. The words in 1 Peter speak to all Christians who pay the price of being Christians in a hostile or indifferent society. The price is indeed great for Christians who work in totalitarian lands. Advancement in one's own profession may be blocked by one's "fanaticism." The discrimination affects the extended family. The Christian not only suffers as a Christian, but brings suffering upon others.

Subtler pressures work in the Western world, where the greatest value of all is tolerance. Tolerance extends to many lifestyles, but it may not extend to the Christian whose commitment is looked upon with disdain. Christian commitment may not stand in the way of advancement, but where it is taken seriously it can make life difficult. People with Christian commitment sometimes ask hard ethical questions of their employers. They place Christ and the church first in their lives, and these demands come into conflict with the absolute loyalty that is expected of the worker. Thus the advice to slaves is not far removed from the world of the twenty-first century, for we too live our Christian lives in unfavorable circumstances.

The significance of the advice to slaves is weakened in the English translations of 2:19, 20. In the Greek of these two verses, there is the repetition of the words, "For this is grace." The RSV renders the words, "For one is approved" and "you have God's approval." The NIV renders the words, "It is commendable." The readers are told twice, "This is grace." The grace of God—his gracious, unmerited gift—is experienced where we live our Christian lives in the midst of difficult circumstances.

At the heart of 1 Peter is the offer of God's grace. In the opening words of the book the readers are offered God's grace: "May grace and peace be multiplied to you" (1:2). Near the end of the book, the readers are told that "this is the grace of God; stand fast in it" (5:12). God's grace was long ago announced by the prophets and is now experienced in the church (1:10). Although grace is experienced already, it is yet to come (1:13) with the coming of the Lord. The exile community, vulnerable as it is in a hostile society, relies on the grace of God to survive. Thus all Christians, including Christian slaves, are told, "This is the grace of God."

The grace of God is not sold at discount prices. Popular religion attempts to convince us that grace is available without a price to be paid. Christianity is sold and marketed as if grace were easily available without cost. Churches compete with each other like merchandisers to offer more benefits at less cost. The epistle of 1 Peter challenges our easy assumptions about faithful Christian commitment, for the epistle rings with the assurance that grace is found where we lose ourselves and even suffer for our faith.

God's Calling

If Christian slaves had thought that their service to God would be greatly enhanced if only they could find another place to serve, they were disappointed by the words of 1 Peter 2:21, "For unto this you were called." Their status, as onerous as it might be, was a place where they could experience God's grace and serve him. Remarkably, their mundane chores are described, not as an unfortunate and temporary circumstance, but as a "calling," an opportunity to serve God.

Normally, God's calling is associated with the invitation to become a Christian (cf. 1 Pet. 1:15; 2:9; 5:10). Sometimes it is associated with a mission to which God commissions us (cf. Gal. 1:15). But in the advice to Christian slaves, the calling was to be exercised at the work place, in the midst of the drudgery and even the misery of slavery.

At times in our history this truth has been rediscovered. There have been times when we spoke of the professions as a "calling," a term derived from the Christian faith. The professions were a calling because they provided a place for service to others. The term suggested that those who were involved in secular professions could be involved in a religious calling as surely as any who were employed in the ministry.

The implication of 1 Peter is not only that a few select professions can be described as a Christian calling, but that every worthwhile task—even that of the household slave—could be seen as a calling. In acts of service to others, in demonstrating that the story of Christ has made an impact on our lives, we are involved in our Christian calling. If slaves could find their calling in unfavorable conditions, Christian teachers, mechanics, attorneys, and salesmen can see in the words of 1 Peter a challenge: "For unto this you were called." We discover the grace of God as we pour out our energies for doing what is right.

Like the slaves of 1 Peter, we come into contact with the non-Christian world in our own professions. Those of us who are involved in full-time work with the church are often deprived of the opportunity to demonstrate our Christian faith as effectively as do those who interact with the world daily. The Christian who takes his calling seriously has an extraordinary opportunity to live out the exile existence at the office or in the classroom. Some who are never exposed to Christian values can be introduced to them only at the job because they come into contact with Christians who have maintained their identity and demonstrated a different kind of lifestyle.

On Having a Story

How do we maintain this Christian identity when we live in this culture and are bombarded daily with its messages? We watch the same television and we read the same books that others read, and we are likely to be absorbing the same messages. We are bombarded with the message daily that we should "look out for number one," develop our own potential, and assert our rights. The role models that are offered in this society are those who climb to the top through single-minded devotion to their own advancement. Maintaining our identity is not an easy matter when we listen to the same messages that our culture hears constantly.

Although ancient Christians did not have the forms of communication that we have today, they had their own version of our problem. As a minority group, they too were bombarded with the values of their own culture. Christian slaves and Christian wives were surrounded by those who did not share their values. From childhood they had heard the tales of heroes who were models of violence and promiscuity. They could not retreat from this world.

When the advice was offered to slaves that they should serve in unfavorable circumstances, the slaves were also offered a strategy for maintaining their identity. "Unto this you were called," they are told. Then in the next line the slaves are reminded of their story. "Because Christ also suffered for you, leaving you an example, that you should follow in his steps." Their neighbors lived by their own stories, but Christians had a story all their own. The words of 2:21-25 summarize the story of Jesus. The passage is similar to 3:17-22, where the instruction to the readers is followed again by the story of the death and victory of Christ. Both passages have a poetic ring to them, as if the words of a song are being quoted. We are told about the one who did not return evil for evil or seek his own rights, but who placed his trust in God alone.

The inclusion of the story in the middle of instructions to Christians is a reminder that the Christian lifestyle grows out of the Christian story. The words are so poetic that they may in fact be known to the readers. Perhaps they were the words of a song that they knew from worship. Without doubt these words were at the center of the Christian proclamation which had been presented at their baptism. Apparently the words were repeated often enough at church that Peter could appeal to Christians by saying, in effect, "Do you not remember our story?" Their story shaped their character and their values. That fundamental message was never something to be left behind. Rather, it was repeated so often that it became their point of orientation as they made moral choices.

An appropriate criticism of much Christian preaching is that it consists almost exclusively of demands and prohibitions. Indeed, the word "preach" often connotes a moralistic speech filled with duties to be performed. The moral injunction of 1 Peter is intimately related to the Christian story. Here Christian morality is more than unconnected commandments. Christian morality is founded on the story that illuminates all of one's moral choices.

Stories have played a role in all ages in shaping identity. Alexander the Great carried with him the stories of the heroes described in Homer's *Iliad* and *Odyssey*. American character has often been shaped by the stories of the great heroes of the past whose deeds are meant to inspire us to imitate them. Christians also live by a story. Unlike the stories which Alexander knew, the Christian story concerns the one who sacrificed himself for others. In Christian worship the story continues to be repeated in sermon and song. If it is told enough, it will tell us what we become when we follow "in his steps."

Christians will be tempted to abandon the story, assuming that it has been heard often enough before. We may conclude that our audiences need something more interesting or entertaining. We are reminded in 1 Peter that Christian character is based on the submissive one. If we forget the story which provides our orientation, no amount of thundering commandments can guide us in becoming the people who know how to make the daily moral decisions that face us.

Questions for Discussion

1. How did slavery in ancient times differ from the slavery in American history?

2. Why did early Christian writers not challenge the institution of slavery?

3. In what way is the advice to slaves the heart of 1 Peter? How is this advice relevant to Christians in very different social situations?

4. Discuss the idea of grace in 1 Peter. Under what circumstances does one experience God's grace? How does this view compare with popular American views of the grace of God?

5. Do Christians commonly view their work as a "calling" that has Christian significance? What are the implications of the advice to slaves for our view of daily work?

6. How do stories shape our values? Discuss the impact of stories in shaping American values. How can Christians be shaped by the one story? What is the role of preaching and music in giving us a story? Does the cross have a direct impact on our decision-making?

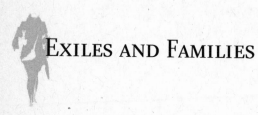

Chapter 8

EXILES AND FAMILIES

"...so that some ... may be won without a word by the behavior of their wives. ..."
1 Peter 3:1-7

In a university class on marriage and the family, Stanley Hauerwas reads a letter to the class describing a family tragedy. He himself has composed the letter, in which he describes a parent's anguish over the son who had disappointed him. At first the son had done very well. He had excelled as a student and an athlete. After serving in the military he had gone to law school, and he had seemed to have a promising future ahead of him. There was even talk of the son's potential for a high political office. However, he had recently joined a religious sect from the East and he had turned his back on his former life and family. Now he seemed to want to have nothing to do with his family. In fact his only ambition was to be of service to his religious brothers and sisters. The family is absolutely heart-sick about this, and they do not know what to do.

Dr. Hauerwas then asks his students who they think wrote the letter. They usually assume that it is from a family whose son has become a Moonie or joined one of the many Hindu sects. He then points out to them that it could have easily been written by a fourth-century Roman family over their son's conversion to Christianity.[1]

That letter could also have come out of the first century. As we read of disciples who followed Jesus' call to "leave father and mother, brother and sister," we easily overlook the pain and the grief that was experienced by those fathers and mothers, brothers and sisters, who must have reacted to the loss of their loved ones with a mixture of shock and horror. The most intimate disciples around Jesus had left everything to follow him. Ancient households must have looked on this new movement in much the same way as we have come to look upon the new cults that separate impressionable young people from their families. Many parents must have grieved, asking what had gone wrong with a Simon or Andrew, a Mary Magdalene or a Joanna. We can only imagine the pain that was involved with the families left behind. We imagine the break with parents, grandparents, cousins and friends whose way of life had been rejected.

As Christianity spread, it continued to divide families. Although entire families were sometimes converted together (cf. Acts 11:14; 16:15, 31; 1 Cor. 1:16), others were not. In some instances masters became Christians without their slaves, as in the case of Philemon. In other instances, slaves became Christians without their masters. Husbands were converted without their wives (1 Cor. 7:12), and wives came to Christ without their husbands (1 Cor. 7:13).

To some, Christianity must have appeared to be a revolutionary institution, a strange cult which separated families and planted strange ideas in the minds of slaves and women. Tacitus' comment about the Jews' practice of dividing families, which is cited in chapter 6,[2] was undoubtedly a familiar charge against Christians.

In ancient times it was unthinkable for a wife not to follow her husband's religion. Years later, Tertullian wrote of the attitude of pagan husbands toward the religion of their Christian wives: "If a vigil has to be attended, the husband, the first thing in the morning, makes her an appointment for the baths; if it is a fast day, he holds a banquet on that very day. If she has to go out, household affairs of urgency at once come in the way."[3]

The resentment of Christians led to rumors about them. We notice in 1 Peter that the Christians were the objects of hostile rumors. They are branded as "evildoers" (2:12; cf. 3:17; 4:15) by their neighbors. Undoubtedly a major source of the slander was the perception that Christians had left old relationships behind, even to the point of rejecting their families.

For Christians, the sharp line dividing them from their families was undoubtedly painful. However, they knew that they found something infinitely more valuable than what they had left behind, for they knew that they had been liberated. In 1:18, they are reminded that they have been "ransomed from the foolish ways inherited from your fathers." Christianity had indeed separated them from the customs and traditions of their families, and this separation was nothing less than a "ransom" or liberation. In place of the old family there was a new "brotherhood" (2:17), a family of believers.

This new situation presented Christians with a serious dilemma. If Christians had been "ransomed from the futile ways inherited from the fathers," how was a Christian wife to react toward her non-Christian husband? Her new religion appeared to be the epitome of insubordination. Should she assert her independence and reject the values of her society? How could she respect and submit to a husband who was still captive in the "futile ways inherited from the fathers?" What impact would Christianity now have on the way she conducted herself as a wife? Wouldn't it be appropriate for her to leave this husband behind until he could share this liberation from old traditions and customs? In this situation, Christian spouses recognized that family life would never be the same for them.

If family life was changed greatly in those mixed marriages, what was the impact of the Christian faith when the entire family was Christian? Apparently some of the Christians of 1 Peter lived with non-Christian spouses, while other families were united in their Christian faith. On the surface, these Christian families must have looked no different from anyone else. Probably all of them asked what this new direction in their lives meant for family life. Perhaps they wondered what it meant to be a holy, exile people in matters of family life.

Christianity and Family Life

What impact does the Christian faith have on our own families? We would like to claim that Christian families are immune from the disease that afflicts family life in contemporary Western culture, but we are deeply concerned that Christian families are struggling from the same instability that threatens families everywhere. The emphasis on marriage enrichment seminars, the popularity of DVD series on the family, and the immense number of books on Christianity and family life indicate that we ask some of the same questions that are raised in 1 Peter. We have models everywhere in our culture for what it means to be a husband or wife, but we want to know what it means to be a husband or wife in Christ. How can Christ have an impact on family life?

The answer in 1 Peter is amazingly brief. It offers little in the way of detail, but it provides important insights for Christian family members today. "Wives, be submissive to your husbands," Christian women are told (3:1). Most of the advice is to wives because apparently wives were more numerous than husbands in this church. The advice that is given is familiar to anyone who has read the epistles of Paul, for there also the word to wives is reduced to the simple instruction, "Be submissive to your husbands" (Eph. 5:22; Col. 3:18). As a matter of fact, the instruction to "be submissive" is deeply rooted throughout the New Testament. Christian family members are to "be submissive" to each other (Eph. 5:21), and Christians are to "be submissive" to every fellow worker (1 Cor. 16:22). In Paul and in 1 Peter, Christians are to "be submissive" to the governing authorities (Rom. 13:1; 1 Pet. 2:13). In 1 Peter, the same verb is used for the Christian's response to governing authorities (2:13), for the Christian slave's attitude toward his master (2:18), and for the Christian wife's response to her pagan husband.

The advice to submit is particularly remarkable in a book that challenges Christians to live as aliens and exiles in a hostile environment, for it seems that Christians are being instructed to adapt to the standards of an environment where submission was always the standard for those who were in an inferior position. Those who were ruled were always expected to be submissive to their rulers. Slaves were always expected to submit to their rulers, and it was always the norm for wives to be submissive to their husbands. Thus Christian wives were expected to respond in the same way that all wives responded to their husbands: to be submissive and to recognize their authority. Indeed, Sarah in her response to Abraham is the model for the Christian wife in her response to her non-Christian husband (1 Pet. 3:6; cf. Gen. 18:12). Thus while the Christian wife has left behind the old traditions of the past (1:18), old relationships continue. Even aliens and exiles find themselves living under the same roof as those who have not left old traditions behind. Here Christian wives live by the standards that are acceptable to their husbands.

The advice about the woman's dress likewise reflects the higher standards of ancient times. Ancient moralists warned against excessive or luxurious dress, for this ostentation was scarcely a sign of the woman's submission. According to 1 Peter, no Christian wife should see her new freedom in Christ as the opportunity to challenge the standards of her time. Christians shared with their neighbors a standard of modesty in dress and demeanor.

This advice reminds us that the morality of exiles is not always opposed to the society in which it lives. Institutions, customs, and laws exist that hold society together. At times Christians conform to the common morality of the day. In the case of 1 Peter, a Christian morality that was consistent with the standards of the time was meant to silence those who suggested that Christianity undermined morality (cf. 2:15).

We may be amazed that a book which tells exile Christians not to fit in to prevailing moral standards also calls on them to "fit in" to some popular standards. However, the advice means more than to "fit in," for the Christian wife did not simply adopt the popular morality of the day. Her membership in a religion that was not her husband's was an act of insubordination, suggesting that her commitment to Christ came first in her life. Nevertheless, she was submissive to the will of her husband where it did not conflict with her faith.

Her submissiveness involved more than "fitting in" to popular standards because submission is an important Christian word, not only for Christian wives, but for the entire Christian community as well. In 3:8, all Christians are to demonstrate "a humble mind." In 5:6, humility is the distinguishing mark of all Christians. Even those who have authority are to renounce the domineering attitude (5:3). Thus Christian wives are challenged to be models of the quality that characterizes all Christians. Her submissiveness is not a matter of "fitting in" to popular standards, but of adopting the new standard of humility that was intended for all Christians.

Behind this advice is the story of the cross. We cannot forget that the advice to Christian slaves was supported by a story of the Submissive One who went to the cross (2:21). According to 1 Peter 2:21, following in the footsteps of Jesus does not only involve a heroic act of martyrdom. One follows in his footsteps within the daily routine of home life. The cross provides a new consciousness where we do not look out only for our own interests, but for the interests of another. The Christian wife's new life in Christ did not prevent her from placing the concerns of her husband above her own. Indeed, the story of the cross provided a new understanding of freedom (cf. 2:16), for now she discovered her freedom within the context of a life of submission.

If pagan neighbors were sometimes won over when they saw the good works of Christians (cf. 2:12), no one had a greater opportunity to see the impact of Christianity on human lives than the spouses of Christians. Thus, non-Christian husbands could be won over when they saw the conduct of their wives. The Christian exiles were constantly observed by their neighbors. Peter's word for "see" in 2:12; 3:1 was the word for close observation, study, and examination. The change in Christian behavior was a matter for close examination. And thus husbands were won over "without a word" because of the impact of Christianity on the conduct of their wives. Christianity had made a difference in families! On the surface, Christian wives might not have looked different from their pagan neighbors, but close scrutiny revealed the change in their lives. They had become more caring and selfless in their attitude toward their husbands. The Christian story had taught them the value of humility, and Christian wives were willing to follow in the footsteps of the one who willingly laid down his life for others. She did not place her own needs at the center of the relationship. Pagan husbands could not have failed to notice that their Christian wives even responded to their domineering, even abusive, behavior with acts of kindness. Those who could not have been won over with persuasive words were won over by selfless lives. Family life was changed by the Christian faith.

Christian Husbands

The advice to husbands in 3:7 reflects the profound difference that Christianity had made for husbands. Pagan husbands assumed their absolute dominance in the household. The subordination of the wife was taken for granted, but with little thought of the reciprocal duties of the husband. In 1 Peter, the duties are reciprocal. Husbands are instructed to "live considerately" with their wives, "bestowing honor on the woman as the weaker sex."

This passage reminds us that the household passages in the New Testament always give reciprocal obligations for husbands and wives (cf. Eph. 5:21-31; Col. 3:18-41). Whereas husbands in Ephesians and Colossians are told to *love* their wives, here they are told to "live considerately" with them. The word rendered "live" (*synoikountes*) means literally to "live together" or "cohabit," and it emphasizes the unity of married life. To live "considerately" (literally "according to knowledge") is to treat one's wife with

95

respect and insight that grows out of love. There is an insight that grows out of love, as Paul says in Philippians 1:9 ("that your love be rich in knowledge"). Indeed, the entire Christian community is distinguished by the consideration that grows out of love. This distinguishing mark of Christian community has a special meaning in the marriage of Christians, for here husband and wife are also brother and sister in Christ. The consideration that Christian believers have for each other thus continues within the Christian family. Indeed, Christian husbands "bestow honor" on their wives (3:7) in the same way that all Christians honor each other (cf. 2:17). Christian husbands, unlike their pagan neighbors, treat their wives with consideration. Like their Christian wives, they do not insist on their own rights and place their spouses at their disposal. Together, both husbands and wives demonstrate selfless care toward each other.

The new insight which must have given Christian husbands a totally new mindset was the fact that husbands and wives are "joint heirs of the grace of life." In Christ all—men and women—make up the "spiritual stones" of God's house (cf. 2:4). All Christians together are recipients of the grace of God (cf. 1:10; 4:10; 5:12), and all are "joint heirs" (cf. Rom. 8:17; Eph. 3:6) of God's promises. When Christian husbands recognized that their wives were "joint heirs" of God's promises and that they prayed together (3:7), undoubtedly they recognized that it would be unthinkable to regard their wives as anything less than their equals. Because they were of equal value as "spiritual stones" in God's house, they were of equal value in the home. This knowledge gave them the new insight that transformed them from their earlier view of a family life based on dominance to a new vision based on the loving consideration of the needs of the other.

Christian Families Today

What is the answer to the gigantic problems facing family life in our own time? Churches throughout the country are showing their deep concern about building Christian families within the church. I am amazed at the quantity of literature on the subject of family. However, I am convinced that we seldom discover the real answer to family life. We borrow the solutions that are offered in our society. It is common for Christian publishers to offer answers to the problems of family life which emphasize communication, sexual technique, conflict management, and many other features that improve relationships. While these topics may be useful, 1 Peter offers a deeper answer. Unless Christian husbands learn the significance of submitting their wills to the will of another, no amount of technique or communication will build a relationship.

What Peter calls for is a special dimension that distinguishes the Christian family from all others. Although non-Christians may often have stable relationships, the Christian faith provides a unique dimension to marriage and family that grows out of the story of the one who gave himself for others. Within this kind of family, personal ambitions and pleasures are sacrificed for the benefit of the relationship. Acts of kindness become habitual for those who have learned to think first of others.

A marriage based on mutual submission is not likely to be popular in a culture that emphasizes personal growth at all costs. Through the media we constantly hear the stories that shape modern consciousness. In the movie, *Kramer vs. Kramer*, a young woman's quest for self-fulfillment leads her to abandon her family. In many of the models offered by the media, the individual who leaves behind old relationships that inhibit his or her growth is the model to be followed.

It is no accident that a culture which finds submission repugnant also does not have the capacity to hold families together. Christian families are uniquely built on the knowledge that we share a life with others who have been loved by Christ. The selfless love which we learned at the cross is shared so that we learn to look to the interests of others in the family. In our culture, Christians who practice this kind of family life will be "aliens and exiles."

NOTES

1   Stanley Hauerwas, "The Family as a School for Character," *Religious Education* 80 (1985), 278.

2   Tacitus, History. V. 5, cited in David Balch, *Let Wives Be Submissive: The Domestic Code of 1 Peter*, SBLMS (Chico, CA: Scholars Press, 1981), 73.

3   Tertullian, Ad Uxor II. 4f, cited in A. Harnack, *The Mission and Expansion of Christianity in the First Three Centuries* (1908; reprint edition, New York: Harper, 1961), 385-395.

Questions for Discussion

1. Describe how families in ancient times would have reacted to the conversion of their members, comparing their reaction with that of families today whose children become converted to a religion not shared by the family.

2. What impact does Christianity have on families today? To what extent are the solutions we have for the crisis in family life secular rather than biblical?

3. Discuss the Christian view of "equality" in the home. To what extent is equality an ideal? To what extent should important decisions in the home be determined jointly? Give some ex-

amples of where submissiveness plays a role in the modern family. In what circumstances is submissiveness carried to an extreme?

4. Discuss the ways in which the advice in 1 Peter can be helpful for Christian families today. Discuss the comment that modern society, with its disdain for submissiveness, lacks the capacity to hold families together.

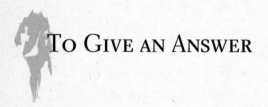

Chapter 9

TO GIVE AN ANSWER

"Now who is to harm you if you are zealous for what is right?"
1 Peter 3:13-22

In William Styron's *Sophie's Choice*, Sophie is a Polish refugee living in Brooklyn, having survived the horrors of the Auschwitz death camp. Of the many memories from the Nazi camp which continue to haunt her, one was the occasion when she, with her blond hair and her command of the German language, had tried to make her life easier by attempting to convince the Nazi commander that she shared his hatred of the Jews and his view of the world. She was willing to say what he wanted to hear out of fear over her fate and the fate of her children. She was willing to repeat all of the Nazi slogans if it could save her children and herself.

Minority groups who live in the midst of a hostile majority commonly feel the pressure to conform to the majority point of view. Under extreme duress, captives begin to express the same sentiments as their captors in time of war. Even victims of kidnapping are known to echo the views of their captors. Immigrants to the United States have tried to blend in to American society as quickly as possible, for we have not always looked kindly on those who persisted in their own ways, particularly when they rejected our way of life.

Flannery O'Connor's short story, "The Displaced Person," is a reminder of the vulnerability of the stranger in our own land. In her story, immigrants from Eastern Europe have come to a little southern town. Mrs. Shortley's suspicions grow like a black thunder cloud when she watches this family of displaced persons.

> With foreigners on the place, with people who were all eyes and had no understanding, who had come from a place continually fighting, where the religion had not yet been reformed—with this kind of people, you had to be on the lookout every minute. She thought there ought to be a law against them. What were they doing over here anyway? . . . And worst of all, they learned the English language.
>
> It gets to be where you can't tell the difference between us and them.[1]

At the end of the story, the displaced persons have to go, for they are perceived as a threat to the way things were. In order to survive, they need to blend into the larger society.

The early Christians had many reasons for wanting to blend into their surroundings at the time when 1 Peter was written, for they had rejected old traditions (1:18; 4:4) and adopted new ones. Their strange ways had led to rumors (2:12), and rumors had led to outbreaks of open hostility. Their neighbors noticed how they remained aloof from the larger populace, and how they had their own "secret meetings." "What are the Christians up to?" was undoubtedly a familiar question. While no organized persecution is evident in 1 Peter, the open hostility is so apparent that violence could erupt at any time. The prospect of "suffering as a Christian" (4:16) or "suffering for righteousness sake" (3:14) was a reality each day.

Even if the Christians did not suffer from mob violence, their neighbors would make their lives difficult through discrimination at work, disregard for their rights, and a general disdain for them. The price of leaving behind the traditions of the past was high. It was the price of the alien existence.

Alien communities face a dilemma which may lead them in one of two ways. One alternative has been to conform to the majority point of view, to blend in with the prevailing ideas. The other alternative has been to withdraw and preserve their identity at all costs. Some alien communities have been so intent on preserving their identity that they have isolated themselves totally from the larger population. Throughout the history of Christianity, communities have chosen to isolate themselves from the corruptions of society by forming communities of their own where their contact with the outside world would be minimal.

How does the church today preserve its own identity in a non-Christian culture? Minority groups can easily be intimidated and fearful because of their point of view. This concern over the impact of intimidation is addressed in the section of 1 Peter that begins with the question, "Now who is to do you harm if you are zealous for what is right?" (3:13). Throughout the preceding section, Christians have been told to counter their hostile neighbors by "doing right" (2:15, 20; 3:6, 11). According to 3:6, Christian wives are told to "do right" and not be afraid. The Christians neither greet hostility with hostility nor retreat to a safe zone where they do not have to encounter hostile neighbors.

This advice leaves the Christians vulnerable and exposed to danger. Thus they are asked, "Now who is to do you harm if you are zealous for the good?" The answer seemed simple enough. Magistrates in city government have the power of life and death. Pagan husbands have the right to do harm to their Christian wives. Non-Christian masters could give incredible punishment to slaves whose Christian commitment appeared to them as insubordination. Outraged family members could do harm to those relatives who had rejected them. From one perspective, there were many who could do harm.

In 1 Peter 3:13, the question is only rhetorical, as the context shows. The implied answer is, "No one can do you harm." Peter has in mind a triumphant answer. The question reminds us of Paul's words in Romans 8:34, "If God is for us, who can be against us?" Isaiah 50:9 has a similar rhetorical question: "Behold, the Lord God helps me, who will declare me guilty?" The answer, as in 1 Peter 3:13, is "no one." That is, because God is present no one has to live in fear. Only a conviction of the power of God prevents the exile community from giving in to its fears.

The fact that "no one can do us harm" does not exclude Christians from the reality of suffering. Slaves suffer unjustly (2:19-20). Christians are reproached for the name (4:16). According to 3:14, even the suffering and discrimination are not a basis for fear, for "if you suffer for righteousness' sake, you will be blessed." The words remind us of the Sermon on the Mount, where Jesus says, "Blessed are those who are persecuted for righteousness' sake, for theirs is the kingdom of heaven" (Matt. 5:10). Throughout 1 Peter, it is assumed that Christians will be tested (1:6-7) by the circumstances in which they live. However, the mood that permeates the book is not one of foreboding, but of the deep joy that Christians find, even in the midst of suffering for their faith (cf. 1:18; 4:13). Those who have the eyes to see know the answer to the question, "Who can do you harm?"

The people of God have always been vulnerable to forces beyond their control. Indeed, faith is the response of those who recognize that there are forces beyond our control. In 3:14-15 the people are challenged: "Have no fear of them, nor be troubled, but in your hearts reverence Christ as Lord." We have an alternative to fear; it is to "reverence Christ as Lord." The words, derived from Isaiah 8:12-16, were once addressed to the people of Israel when the Assyrian armies threatened to destroy their nation, and terror was spreading among them. Isaiah had said to them, "Do not call conspiracy what they call conspiracy, and do not fear what they fear, nor be in dread. But the Lord of hosts, him you should regard as holy; let him be your fear, and let him be your dread." Because we reverence God as the Lord of history, we see beyond the fear and intimidation of the moment.

To Give an Answer

The remarkable challenge to be "always prepared to make a defense" (3:15) could only be possible within a community which had discovered that God is the Lord of history. Only a community that could "reverence Christ as Lord" rather than fear its hostile neighbors could take on the challenge of giving a defense of its views, for such a defense involved risks. In order to be able to give an answer, the alien community would interact daily with its hostile neighbors rather than retreat into an enclave of its own. Those who would ask about the reason for their hope would undoubtedly ask in a mocking or condescending way (cf. 3:16). The Christian might even pay a price for his answer, as it might result in ridicule or punishment (3:17). Nevertheless, Christians are neither to tell their hostile neighbors what they want to hear nor to retreat behind walls where they would never have to defend their faith. Such a courageous response was possible only for those who had learned to fear God rather than their hostile neighbors.

Perhaps evangelism resulted when courageous Christians made their defense at the work place, in the market place, or in the neighborhood. Hostile questioners could have heard more than rumors. We may assume that Christians were regularly asked to explain their behavior. Peter challenges the Christians to set the record straight, to correct misconceptions of their morality, clarify their motives, and describe their hope.

The challenge to "give an answer" was given to the whole community, and not only to its leaders. Every Christian was expected to put into words his religious beliefs and to be able to articulate the convictions that provided the foundation for his existence.

The word for "defense" (KJV: "reason") was the term commonly used for a defense speech in court. It is the term used by Paul in his defense speeches in Acts (22:1; 25:16). Paul uses the word in 1 Corinthians 9:3, when he says, "This is my defense to those who would examine me." In 2 Timothy 4:7 (cf. Phil. 1:7, 16) it is used for Paul's defense in court. The term suggests a reasoned statement, an ability to put one's convictions into words.

The challenge to the exile community was to speak courageously and thoughtfully about its faith. Without the strong convictions that could be put into words, it would be in danger of assimilating once more into its environment.

Donald Baillie once preached a sermon on 1 Peter 3:15 entitled, "Intelligent Christianity," where he made a plea for a Christianity that has "to some extent thought itself out, and knows what it means and believes, and can give answers to the world's pathetic questions."[2] He suggests that one major source of the power of early Christianity was that Christians knew where they stood and were able to articulate their faith. In the sermon he quotes the words of the great classical scholar, T. R. Glover, who argued that Christianity was triumphant because Christians "read about Jesus, and they knew him, and they knew where they stood. . . . Who did the thinking in that ancient world? Again and again it was the Christian. He out-thought the world."[3]

From the defense given by ordinary Christians there developed the task of the "apologists" of the second century. Their task was to make a reasoned statement of the faith before their detractors. The great apologists of the second century wrote intellectual defenses of the Christian faith to Roman rulers in an attempt to meet pagan culture's criticism that Christianity was a new superstition. Christianity never hid in a corner, and the Christians were not afraid to articulate their faith.

This defense is to be done with "meekness and fear" (3:16-17). The Christian is not motivated by fear of the sneering questioner (cf. 3:14), but by the fear of the God who is the Lord of history. Christians are not called upon to answer with ridicule or to invite hostility with their answers, nor to answer sneering questioners with sneering answers. Indeed, Christians are known both for their thoughtful answers and their demeanor in answering. Just as a Christian wife may win over her pagan husband "without a word," the Christian at the work place or in the neighborhood may silence his critics by courageous answers that respond to hostility with grace and meekness. It was not enough to give an intelligent answer in an arrogant demeanor. Christians were expected to be known for both their reasoned answers and the humble demeanor (cf. 3:8-12).

One may wonder if some sneering questioners soon became Christians when their questions were met with reasoned answers given with extraordinary self-control. Our records from the second century indicate that the power of Christianity was often seen in the way Christians faced the hostility. Paul was only the first of many persecutors who was won to Christ. Pagan neighbors were deeply impressed at the Christians' response to persecution. At times even Roman soldiers were won over. When we consider that Christianity grew in the presence of hostility, we must imagine that many jeering questioners became Christians when they heard serious answers to their questions.

Strategies for Today

The temptation for Christianity in the twenty-first century, as in the first and second centuries, is to tell our culture what it wants to hear. I was told recently of a church that took neighborhood surveys to find out what people want in a church. The answers were meant to shape the church's mission. We have seen churches whose agenda is shaped by left-wing political causes and by right-wing political causes. During a recent election, an editorial in a church bulletin indicated that the message of that church "just happened" to coincide with the agenda of one of the major political parties! Churches often "just happen" to proclaim our culture's answers to some of the deepest problems that face us, providing only a weak echo of what others are saying.

The search for relevance may motivate us to be listening to our culture's questions and to be framing our answers in a way that they will be acceptable to our listeners. However, such attempts to be relevant often invite only the scorn of the secular world. Those who find this Christianity acceptable to their own worldview must ask why they should bother to consider being a Christian when Christianity provides only a poor echo of popular values.

In 1971, Peter Berger wrote a prophetic article in *The Christian Century*, in which he tried to envision what might lie ahead for American Christianity. He noted a loss of self-confidence in Protestantism, and an anxiety about the future. Does Christianity have a future? he asked. He answered that the Christianity that is always *listening* to the modern world's answers will have no future at all. He said that "for some twenty years now we have been fascinated by the question, What does the modern man have to say to the church?" But it is time to ask, What does the church have to say to modern man?[4] He added that ages of faith are marked by the proclamation of those who firmly believe that "they have grasped some important truths about the human condition."[5] His challenge is a reminder that the strength of Christianity comes from its confidence in the power of its message.

One can imagine the courage it took for Christians in the first century to "give a reason for the hope" that was in them and the impression it made on their neighbors when ordinary people could articulate the principles of their faith. If our own age is similar in many respects to the world of 1 Peter, a similar response from Christians today would also have an impact on our society. This kind of response presupposes that whole communities know their story. The story has been told and repeated enough times that every person can tell it. If contemporary churches are serious about "giving an answer," the task of preaching and teaching will be taken seriously. The goal of the Sunday school program will be to ensure that the story has been absorbed by the entire church; and the youth program will be directed toward equipping adolescents so that they can understand their own faith and articulate it for a secular world.

When Christianity triumphed in the ancient world, it could only meet adversity because of its confidence in its message and its awe before the God who had called them. In the modern world, churches often respond to modern culture as if the Christian message is an embarrassment to be hidden away while we reach people with words that they want to hear. First Peter reminds Christians of the power involved when Christians can articulate what they believe.

Because of Christ

We answer clearly and boldly, unafraid of the consequences, because our story still has power over our lives. Before we faced a hostile culture, Christ was the suffering one. In the middle of Peter's advice on behavior (3:13-17), he returns to the story of the suffering Christ in order to remind Christians who they are. Before they suffered, Christ suffered. But the suffering of Christ did not end with defeat, but with his new status at the right hand of God (3:22). It is not accidental that the story in 3:18-22 begins with "for." The little word connects the fate of Christians with the fate of Christ, and it reminds them that the path to suffering ultimately ends in triumph. It is no wonder, then, that the readers are asked earlier (3:13), "Who can do you harm?" The answer is "no one," because the future has been guaranteed. As one scholar has said, "The way of suffering for the sake of Christ has become a victory processional and a way of blessing."[6]

For centuries Christians have debated the meaning of the puzzling words of 3:19, and the debate is likely to continue. But we should not lose sight of the impact of 1 Peter 3:18-22. The passage is poetic, and it tells the entire story of Christ. Its major point is that Christ has won the victory. In so doing, no one was omitted from the triumphant message—even the spirits in prison heard it. Christ is victorious! And now Christians, through baptism, share in the security of belonging to Christ, whose suffering ended in glory. When Christians are equipped with this song, they will have the courage to offer a "reason for their hope" to everyone who asks.

The path of assimilation is for those who have lost confidence that the Christian story retains its power. The Christianity that survives in a non-Christian land will be deeply rooted in its story.

NOTES

1 Flannery O'Connor, "The Displaced Person," in *The Complete Stories* (New York: Farrar, Straus & Giroux, 1971).

2 Donald Baillie, *To Whom Shall We Go?* (New York: Scribner's, 1955), 59.

3 Cited in Baillie, 63.

4 Peter Berger, "A Call for Authority in the Christian Community," *Christian Century* September 27, 1971, p. 1261.

5 Ibid., 1262.

6 L. Goppelt, *Der erste Petrusbrief* (Göttingen: Vandenhoeck und Ruprecht, 1978), 264.

Questions for Discussion

1. Sociologists have shown that much of what we "know" has been socially determined; i.e., we know things because no one disputes them, absorbing from our environment the common assumptions. In what way are our Christian convictions socially determined? What can we expect to happen in a non-Christian society?

2. What options are commonly considered by those who hold the minority point of view? What is the advice in 1 Peter to

those who might be intimidated in holding views that did not fit in with the dominant views?

3. How can the church prepare its people to "make a defense" of their faith? Is this task best done with the Sunday school and preaching?

4. Discuss the comment that Christianity "out-thought" the rest of the world, and that it was victorious because it provided intelligent answers. To what extent is educating the membership a major mission of the church?

5. People often debate whether church growth is enhanced most when it offers a message that society wants to hear or when it offers a distinctly Christian message. What have our experiences indicated?

Chapter 10

EXILE COMMUNITIES

"As each has received a gift, employ it for one another."
1 Peter 4:1-11

Returning missionaries and visitors from other countries frequently express their amazement at the extraordinary resources that are available to modern American churches. Those who dream of having a building of their own and a measure of financial independence are amazed to see urban churches that have the resources to build impressive buildings complete not only with a spacious sanctuary, but also with facilities equipped to serve practically every need and every constituency. A multi-million dollar structure may have an education wing with the latest in audio-visual equipment; a gymnasium for the many activities of the church community; and a kitchen and banquet area capable of providing for a large church. Its resources are also seen in the professional staff which oversees the various ministries of the church. A church of two hundred may have two salaried staff members. A church of five hundred will probably have more.

These developments are very new in modern church life. The increase in the size of the church staff and in the size of the church building reflects the increasing affluence of our entire society and the rise in our expectations. Today we are not satisfied with education programs that show a lack of professionalism, and we expect facilities that correspond to what we see at home or at work. Our increasing affluence has provided us with the resources to alter much of the fabric of church life.

Anyone who has observed the changes in the last generation will notice how vastly church life has changed as a result of our increased expectations. We can hope that our increased resources and our rising expectations have provided us the opportunity to reach out in ways that were impossible in the past.

A church with a strong sense of mission may be able to use these resources in areas of service that would have been impossible without them. The expenditure of vast sums of money may reflect the health, vitality, and commitment of the churches. However, it also raises important questions about our church life. Christians easily become consumers of the services that churches offer, and churches then become involved in a competition for members. Under these circumstances, churches begin to plan their programs with an eye to beating the competition. In some cases, churches have incurred massive indebtedness in order to provide the services that will attract the mass of consumers, knowing that church members migrate from place to place in search of the congregation offering the most services. The competition may also send the church in search of a stellar cast of professional staff members, for the best pulpit personality, the best youth minister, and the best education program may be necessary to attract the people who will pay off the massive indebtedness. Market forces continue to be at work under these circumstances. Salaries escalate, for churches enter into competition with each other in the search for talent. If the consumers are not kept satisfied, they can always find another community that offers more. If the stellar cast does not produce the desired results, the same market forces that escalated the salaries can be at work to terminate those who do not produce.

Vernard Eller, in his book, *The Outward Bound*, contrasted two models that churches employ in determining their future. One is the "caravan" and the other is the "commissary." In a caravan, a group of people make common cause in reaching their destination. A commissary "is an institution which has been commissioned to dispense particular goods, services, or benefits to a select constituency."[1] People come to the commissary to receive the benefits that it provides. Where the church is a commissary, it dispenses everything but demands little in return. Its members look to it for grace, salvation, and fellowship. Membership has its privileges.

If the church is a commissary that exists to meet the requirements of the consumers, is it different from other communities only to the extent that it dispenses grace and salvation? In what sense is the church a new kind of community where God's world has broken through our human way of thinking, and in what sense is the church different from other communities that exist to increase their power and influence?

Before and After (4:1-6)

The exile community of 1 Peter was encouraged to recognize that it was a new kind of community. In 1 Peter 4:1-6, Peter reiterates what the experience of conversion meant in the isolated communities of Asia Minor. Conversion involved a new "mindset" (4:1), which was shared by the rest of the community. Indeed, their lives were divided between "the time that is past" (4:3) and the way they live "now" (4:4). The new existence is characterized by a lifestyle that makes them strangers in their own land. One can translate 4:4, "They think it strange that you do not now join them in the same wild profligacy, and they will abuse you." One can imagine the hostility of the local citizens who noticed that their neighbors no longer attended the festivals and the celebrations in which idolatry and sexual indulgence were common. It was as if the Christians were unpatriotic! The suffering of the Christians, which is referred to in 4:1, came from the discrimination and the hostility of their neighbors who noticed that the Christians had given up their "licentiousness, passions, drunkenness, revels, carousing, and lawless idolatry." One can imagine the disturbances that were created by the new moral commitments. Christian wives would not want to attend with their non-Christian husbands. Neighbors and colleagues would no longer attend together. Old friendships would be strained and then die as the Christians maintained their distance from the old way of life. The Christian community was different from the other communities, for their conversion brought with it a new lifestyle.

Because Christians did not attend the civic festivals, they were soon labeled as "the enemy of mankind."[2] One writer in the third century complained, "You do not go to our shows, you have no part in our processions, you are not present at our public banquets, you shrink in horror from our sacred games."[3] What pagans disliked was that Christians practiced a "new morality," a morality known for its rejection of pagan vices. All other communities joined, but the Christians were different. They were a moral community.

Ancient society's resentment of this moral community is suggested in 4:12-19, a passage that resumes the epistle's theme of the suffering of God's people (cf. 1:6-7; 3:13-14; 5:9). In a pagan culture, suffering will be no stranger to the Christian community (4:12). The suffering may come in the form of insults (4:13), as their neighbors give them the name "Christ-lackeys" ("Christians," 4:16),[4] as if they were a dangerous cult. Apparently their neighbors even question their morality with scurrilous charges, as 4:15 suggests.[5] Christians respond in the knowledge that they share in the sufferings of Christ (4:13) and in the firm hope that in the judgment which they are already experiencing their joy will be complete (4:13) and their tormenters will meet their end. This hope motivates the Christian community to maintain its way of "doing what is right" (4:19), even when these moral commitments are ridiculed by their society. The exile community was no commissary for those who wanted grace without cost.

A New Community (4:7-11)

The new life of Christians involved far more than the renunciation of old traditions and old vices from former times. The new existence involved a community life where individuals from diverse ethnic and socio-economic backgrounds came together, knowing that they were the "living stones" which comprised the house of God (2:4-5). They had nothing in common except their commitment to the one who had died on a cross. And thus as exiles they came together for mutual support. Ancient observers must have been amazed to see a community formed neither by kinship nor by common economic pursuits.

The most astounding fact about this new community was the quality of its life together, for conversion introduced the Christians to a new kind of community, as 1 Peter 4:7-11 indicates. The urgency of maintaining their community is suggested in the instruction to "keep sane and sober for your prayers" (4:7). In corporate prayer the members not only maintain their relationship to God, but with each other as well, just as husbands and wives are brought closer together in their joint prayers (3:7). The new quality of community life is especially indicated by the threefold repetition in this paragraph of the single expression "one another" (4:8, 9, 10). The distinctive feature of the Christian lifestyle is seen not only in what they have renounced, but also in the way their lives are turned toward one another. The church is not the commissary that dispenses grace, but a community that is distinguished by the reciprocal sharing of gifts.

The most important feature of their community life ("above all," 4:8) for one another is the love (*agape*) that binds the community together (cf. "brotherly love" [*philadelphia*] in 1:22; 3:8). The Christians are drawn together as a family, and they are to "love the brotherhood" (2:17). This challenge to love members of the community is undoubtedly the most pervasive instruction in the New Testament. It is found not only in 1 Peter, but throughout the letters of Paul and other writers as well.[6] The modern reader may be surprised to note that the exhortations to love in the New Testament are always directed to members of the community, and not to outsiders.[7] This fact is indicated in 1 Peter 2:17, where the readers are told, "Honor all men. Love the brotherhood. Fear God. Honor the emperor." Christians "do good to all men" (Gal. 6:10), but they love one another. As the frequent use of the word "beloved" indicates, love was the term reserved for a unique relationship within the family. The modern reader is likely to be amazed to see the tone of intimacy that distinguishes the letters of the New Testament.

Paul writes to the Philippians, "For God is my witness, how I yearn for you all with the affection of Christ Jesus" (1:8). He says that the Thessalonians "love all the brethren throughout Macedonia" (3:10). Conversion involved the new reality of *agape* within the community. "The early church's most beautiful word for the new reality which spread in the community given by God is *agape* (love)."[8] It communicated the special care that family members showed to each other. The exile community, whose members now were "homeless" (*paroikos*) because of the gospel, had found a new home (*oikos*) in the community.[9] Ancient people were amazed by the quality of their care for one another. More than a century after 1 Peter, Tertullian recalled that their neighbors were saying of the Christians, "see how they love one another."[10]

Nothing indicates the unique dimension of early Christian community life than the injunction which follows: "Practice hospitality ungrudgingly to one another" (4:9), the second of the "one another" passages. For modern readers, this injunction may not seem remarkable, for we think of hospitality as the natural practice of entertaining our friends. But the word for hospitality (*philoxenia*) meant literally "friendship with strangers." It was the word that was used for entertaining strangers in one's home. We are reminded here that the house was the usual meeting place for Christians. They depended on those who would open their homes to the congregation. Congregational life revolved around homes where traveling Christians knew they could find a place. Missionaries also knew that in each new city homes would be open to them. In two different cities we are told of the church that met in the home of Aquila and Priscilla (Rom. 16:3-5; 1 Cor. 16:19). As they traveled from city to city on business, they appear to have opened their home always.

When we recall the household setting of early Christianity, we can understand the intimacy with which Christians spoke of each other as brothers and sisters. This household setting is also the background for the greeting in Romans 16:13, when he says, "Greet Rufus . . . and his mother and mine." The frequent references to fellow Christians as "beloved" and the injunction to love the brethren are especially intelligible in the context of the household. The regular practice of hospitality allowed the exile community to take on the intimacy that is found only in the best of families. The Christian exiles always had a place of refuge when Christians practiced hospitality. Their pagan neighbors ridiculed them for their vulnerability to fraud as they saw the Christian willingness to accept strangers.

This epistle does not stand alone in the high value it places on hospitality (*philoxenia*, literally "friendship with strangers"). Romans 12:13 commends hospitality for all members. Hebrews 13:2 encourages this practice. One qualification of a bishop was that he be exemplary in hospitality (cf. 1 Tim. 3:2). When we recall the frequent occasions in early Christianity where Christians met in homes and broke down social barriers at common meals, we recognize the role that hospitality must have played in the life of the early church. Some historians argue that the expansion of the early church would have been impossible without the role which hospitality played.[11]

We occasionally see glimpses of the significance of hospitality in the contemporary church, especially where Christians live as exiles. Before the fall of the Berlin Wall, I visited a small congregation in Zagreb, one of the first Churches of Christ in the former Yugoslavia. The local congregation had purchased a residence in the center of the city as a place of worship. In this land where Christianity was officially discouraged, Christians knew the meaning of an exile existence. They found strength in being a community of exiles, for they came together for worship on Sunday and met together for meals at other times during the week. This community, composed largely of those who were now separated from the values of their families, became the extended family. As many as nineteen keys circulated among the members, who regarded this house as a second home.

In my travels, I frequently encountered exile communities whose members taught me the meaning of hospitality. In Germany, Frau Dina Luik is one of my most unforgettable examples. She and her husband Emil, who had been disabled during combat in World War II, were people of modest means. Nevertheless, in the university city of Tuebingen, where people came to study from every continent, any visitor who came to the little house church could expect to be invited into the Luik home for a grand banquet. People received the Luik hospitality, which extended beyond the circle of friends.

The third "one another" passage in Peter's advice reminds us that in these communities every member had a gift, and that gifts were to be employed "for one another." The passage reminds us of Paul's teaching about the body of Christ (1 Cor. 12), as it suggests members bring different gifts for the community. Some have the gift of speaking, and others have the gift of serving. Probably other gifts were present, but only two are mentioned here. What is most important here is not the number of gifts, but the fact that the entire community brought gifts for the benefit of others. The work of the church is not left to the professionals who offer their expertise, but to members who bring to the community what they can.

Vernard Eller has written that two opposing models of church life compete with each other today. In one model, he says, the church is regarded as the Royal Vienna String Quartet. In the other model, the church is a Barbershop Quartet. On the one hand, the purpose of the Vienna Quartet is to produce music of the highest possible quality for the enjoyment of the audience. The goal of this quartet is perfection. On the other hand, the goal of the Barbershop Quartet is the enjoyment of singing.[12] In some churches the goal is the professionalism that satisfies the audience, while in others the goal is the instruction and service of those who offer their own gifts.

Eller also says that the very idea of church "membership" has been distorted, for now "member" means something like "card carrier," someone who has been certified to enjoy the privileges of the institution.[13] Where the New Testament speaks of membership, however, we are described as members of the body of Christ who have an indispensable function for the vitality of the organism. This is the kind of community that is envisioned in 1 Peter 4:10-11.

The strategy for the exile community was not to offer ancient people the commissary which dispensed benefits, but a new kind of community where the members were like family members who gave what they had to preserve the bond of affection. Christians were distinguished not only by their separation from civic life, but by the quality of their community life. It was distinguished by the place of "one another" in the new mindset of the Christians.

Although resources of the church in an affluent society may be remarkable, the economic resources alone will not build strong communities. In a post-Christian land, 1 Peter offers the challenge for congregations to be a new kind of community distinguished by love, hospitality, and mutual service.

NOTES

1 Vernard Eller, *The Outward Bound: Caravaning as the Style of the Church* (Grand Rapids: Eerdmans, 1980), 12.

2 Cited in Robert Wilken, *The Christians as the Romans Saw Them* (New Haven: Yale University Press, 1984), 66.

3 Minucius Felix, Octavius 12, cited in Wilken, 66.

4 Cf. John Elliott, *A Home for the Homeless: A Social-Scientific Criticism of 1 Peter, Its Situation and Strategy* (Philadelphia: Fortress, 1981), 95, on the origin of the name "Christian" as a term of abuse ("Christ-lackey," p. 142).

5 On the charges against Christian morality, see Wilken, 17.

6 Cf. Rom. 14:15; 1 Cor. 4:21; 8:1; 13:1, 2, 3, 4, 8, 13; 14:1; 16:24; 2 Cor. 2:4, 8; 8:7, 8, 24; Gal. 5:13; Phil. 2:1, 2; 1 Thess. 3:12; Philem. 5, 7, 9.

7 Cf. Gerhard Lohfink, *Jesus and Community: The Social Dimension of Christian Faith* (Philadelphia: Fortress, 1982), 110.

8 Lohfink, 109.

9 Elliott, *A Home for the Homeles*, 150, has noted the contrast between *paroikos* (literally "homeless") in 2:11 (RSV "exiles") and *oikos* ("house") in 2:5; 4:17.

10 Tertullian, Apology. xxxix.

11 Adolf Harnack, *The Mission and Expansion of Christianity in the First Three Centuries* (1908; reprint edition, New York: Harper, 1961), 177f.

12 Eller, *The Outward Bound*, 21.

13 Ibid., 13.

Questions for Discussion

1. Has a consumer mentality invaded the church, causing churches to adapt market strategies to attract members? What could the local church leadership do to counteract this consumer mentality?

2. What is the distinction between the church as commissary and as caravan? How would you describe your own congregation?

3. Describe the community life reflected in 1 Peter 4:7-11. In what sense was the church, as an extended family, to be compared to present communities? Does our exile existence bring us together into genuine community life? What factors do our congregations have to overcome in becoming true communities?

4. Community life was a powerful attraction to the rootlessness of ancient societies. In what way could the local church be an attraction to uprooted and lonely people today?

5. Compare the teaching on gifts in 1 Peter with Paul's instructions in 1 Corinthians 12. In what way has the concept of "membership" been distorted in the contemporary church? What did "membership" mean in 1 Corinthians 12?

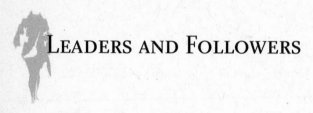

Chapter 11

LEADERS AND FOLLOWERS

"Tend the flock of God, which is your charge."
1 Peter 5:1-5

During the Watergate controversy a syndicated columnist recalled that the interior of the White House had undergone a major renovation during the 1940s, giving this majestic building new conveniences and the amenities of a new age. Thus the White House of the modern era was hardly the White House of Lincoln, Wilson, and Roosevelt. Would it have mattered, asked the columnist, if the White House of Nixon were indeed the same as the White House where Lincoln had sat? Would the modern president have been awed to think that he was sitting where his heroes had struggled over the fate of the nation? The columnist wondered if the sights, smells, and atmosphere of the old White House could possibly have served as a reminder of the dignity of that office and a deterrent to the abuse of the highest office in the country.

Perhaps the columnist overestimated both the goodness of previous leaders and the extent to which present leaders abused this high office, for power and office have always offered their own temptations. Our age is probably not unique in having leaders who abuse power and the privileges of office. What may be unique to our age is the information about leaders at our disposal and the glare of the spotlight which exposes their deceit or incompetence. This information is often accompanied by a deep distrust and cynicism in the populace about leadership and those who hold public office. Public office, as a result, has lost much of the esteem that it once held.

This loss of the respect for the office results in a crisis of leadership that will affect the public in significant ways. For example, office holders who do not expect to be held to the highest standards of trustworthiness will find little motivation to maintain these standards. In addition, when leadership has little respect, those who combine the genuine leadership qualities of ability and trustworthiness will not be inclined to assume the duties of office.

The church increasingly faces a crisis of leadership. Some aspects of our own crisis may be related to our culture's distrust of office holders and leaders. Other aspects of this problem may be unique to the church. Nevertheless, the result is the same. Many good people will not accept the responsibilities of leadership. Church members do not regard the leadership with the esteem and respect that one would expect. The titles "pastor," "elder," "deacon," and "minister" are hardly the goals toward which many members aspire.

In many instances, churches address the crisis of leadership by turning to the techniques of management offered by the corporate world. Here they may choose from a wide variety of management solutions to the problems of leadership. However, what is lacking in the church is not technique, but a basic understanding of what makes leadership Christian.

First Peter and Christian Leadership

When 1 Peter was written to the Christians of Asia Minor in the late first century, the churches in these cities faced imminent peril. The epistle, written to challenge all of the Christian readers to "stand fast" in a time of testing (5:12), addresses some of its words to Christian leaders (5:1-4) and Christian followers (5:5). The "older men" and the "younger men" of 1 Peter have reciprocal responsibilities toward each other. Within these scattered congregations, some were expected to lead in this hour of crisis. Others were expected to recognize and respect the leaders. In this hour of crisis, the church needed the unique gifts of those who were prepared to offer guidance. It also needed those who would accept the guidance that these leaders provided. The church was not meant to face the future as a leaderless mob, but as a community which respected the authority of leadership.

The distinction between the role of the elders and that of other members did not mean that a hierarchy of importance was being established in the church, for the entire letter is addressed to all members who are the "living stones" of God's house (2:5). Indeed, according to 1 Peter 4:10, everyone has received a gift from God. The gift of some is to lead.

The elders who are addressed in 1 Peter are not, as one might conclude from the contrast to the "younger men" in 5:5, merely the "older men" of the congregation who are recognized for their longevity in the church. The awesome responsibilities of the elders listed in 5:1-4 indicate that they hold an office that is apparently reserved for the older men who are capable of fulfilling the duties that are described. The "elder" had a distinguished place in Jewish life. The elders comprised the circle of wise men who governed the affairs of the synagogue and community life. The title was then used as a term for leaders in the Christian communities (cf. Acts 11:30). Acts of the Apostles speaks of the ordination of elders "in every church" (14:23). The epistle to Titus speaks of elders "in every city" (1:5). The elders of biblical times were the primary teachers of the church (1 Tim. 5:17). Like the Jewish synagogues before them, the early congregations turned to a group of older men who were able to lead the community. These were men of wisdom, learning, and experience.

From its beginning, the church was not a democratic institution whose future was determined by the will of the majority. It could face the future securely only when it had men of wisdom to guide it.

The Cost of Leading

The significance of the elders for the life of the church is nowhere more graphically demonstrated than in the words that precede Peter's instructions to elders. Here, in the only reference that the writer makes to himself in the body of the letter (for references to himself in the introduction and conclusion, cf. 1:1; 5:13), he proudly refers to himself as a "fellow elder and witness of the sufferings of Christ" (5:1). While we do not know whether Peter served as an elder of a local congregation or simply shared the functions of an elder on a wider scale, we notice that he identified with elders and proudly accepted the title for himself. He was one of many elders who shared the task of leading God's people.

One can only imagine how ancient elders responded upon seeing the significance that Peter gave their work. Individuals in society may not regard the work of elder in great esteem, but the apostle saw their work as part of his own. To be an elder is to share the work of leading God's people with the apostles! If

Peter's self-designation is taken seriously in the churches, elders in every generation will regard their title with awe.

If the office has dignity, the status is accompanied by the price which the elder must pay. It is no accident that Peter's self-designation "elder" is accompanied by another phrase to describe himself: "witness of the sufferings of Christ." To be a "fellow elder" was also to be a fellow "witness to the sufferings of Christ," for all Christian leadership is accompanied by a price to be paid. Just as the leadership of Christ was unthinkable without his suffering (cf. 3:18), those who point the way in following him demonstrate their willingness to share his sufferings (cf. 4:13).

When the apostle Paul wanted to demonstrate his credentials as a Christian leader, he reminded the Ephesian elders that for three years he "did not cease night or day to admonish everyone with tears" (Acts 20:31). He had given them a living example of the toil and the pain that is required to lead the people of God in order that they could continue his example (cf. Acts 20:32). In another passage, he indicates that what distinguished his leadership style was not his charisma, but his "anxiety for the churches" (2 Cor. 11:28).

To be an elder is to share an esteemed title with the great leaders of the church. One could easily be awed by the list of those who have accepted the title and the responsibility of the elder. The distinguishing mark of God's leaders has been that they were "witnesses of the sufferings of Christ" who were willing to pay a price.

The Job Description of an Elder

What is the job description of an elder? The crisis in leadership is nowhere more apparent than in our uncertainty about the elder's essential task. Is the elder a member of a corporate board whose task is to dispose what others propose? The instructions in 1 Peter are amazingly simple: "Tend the flock of God that is your charge" (5:2 RSV). The NIV renders the instruction, "Be shepherds of God's flock." The NIV accurately captures the essence of the elder's task, as it is indicated in 1 Peter: the task of the elder is "to shepherd." The Greek verb translated "tend" in the RSV (*poimainete*) means literally "tend, lead to pasture." The same task is also mentioned in Paul's final address to the Ephesian elders in Acts 20:28: "Take heed to yourselves and to all the flock, in which the Holy Spirit has made you overseers to tend the flock of God."

The image of the shepherd was as old as it was graphic to the residents of the Near Eastern communities. Israel's most beloved psalm celebrates God as the shepherd who has a shepherd's task:

> He makes me lie down in green pastures,
> He leads me beside still waters;
> He restores my soul.

The shepherd, in this dry land, led his sheep to water and protected them from danger. The Old Testament distinguishes between those shepherds who fail to tend their flocks and those who conscientiously tend those in their charge (cf. Jer. 23:4). According to a number of New Testament passages, Jesus is himself the shepherd (cf. John 10; 1 Pet. 2:25). Jesus also commissions those who will act as shepherds. To the apostles Jesus said, "Tend my sheep" (John 21:16).

This rich imagery is a reminder of the awesome task of the elder. Like the apostle before him, he is a shepherd working on behalf of the chief shepherd. Thus his task is to guide, nurture, and protect the vulnerable flock against its enemies.

The image of the shepherd is a reminder that the task of the elder is to provide nutrition for the flock. The most fundamental task of the elder is to know and understand the Christian faith, to recognize the dangers posed by the "fierce wolves," and to pay the price of protecting the flock. Thus the elder is primarily a teacher who can guide the church in the midst of danger. In the church addressed in 1 Peter, the perilous times required men of faith, learning, and wisdom who were equipped to lead the church. The church, composed of "newborn babes" and others who were struggling to live out their commitments, needed the guidance of older men who had distinguished themselves as teachers.

In our understanding of the elder's task, something has been lost from the perspective of 1 Peter. The elder's task, in the common view, has been increasingly separated from that of providing spiritual nurture. While the professional staff offers expertise in important areas, it is likely that the increasing reliance on the professional staff has been accompanied by the decreasing significance of elders as shepherds who provide direction for the flock of God.

The Dangers of Leadership

Awesome tasks are often accompanied by great temptations. The elder has, as 1 Peter suggests, temptations that are uniquely his, for the authority and respect that are given to him can easily be abused. Thus the three negative clauses in 1 Peter 5:2-3 are reminders of the temptations faced by elders.

We are not sure what temptation is envisioned by the first negative clause, "not by constraint but willingly." The phrase reminds us of Paul's plea to Philemon in the case of Onesimus, the runaway slave. Paul preferred to "do nothing without your consent but of your own free will." He wanted not only Philemon's compliance with Paul's decision, but also his agreement.

The author of Hebrews speaks of the leaders in the church that he addressed, and he indicated that it is not only important to find men who will serve but who will also serve "joyfully, and not sadly" (13:17). Perhaps this is what Peter's advice addresses. The future of the church is assured only when men are willing to accept the inconveniences, the burdens, and even the sleepless nights that accompany leadership. A church that produces no capable men who will find joy in leading will have no future.

The second temptation of leadership concerns money: "not for shameful gain but eagerly." Apparently the leaders of ancient churches had great temptations in the handling of money, for they supervised the offerings and were themselves paid for their services (cf. 1 Cor. 9:7-12). It was beyond dispute that "the laborer is worthy of his hire," for the Lord himself had given this instruction (cf. Luke 10:7). It was expected that those who taught would receive gifts from their pupils (Gal. 6:6). Indeed, the elders of the ancient church were to be paid for their labor in teaching and preaching (1 Tim. 5:17).

Money had its own temptations, as the warnings in 1 Peter and 1 Timothy 3:3 indicate. There was always the danger that the payment and the handling of significant sums of money would attract men for the wrong reason. As men who both received and controlled significant sums, it was necessary that they maintain the highest standards of accountability in this place of trust.

Money still provides temptations in the church. Elders and ministers are tempted to forget that the funds belong to God. Wherever men are paid for their services as laborers worthy of their hire, they must resist the temptation to work "for shameful gain." The corporate models, in which one's pay is commensurate to his value in the marketplace, has no place in the church. Nor is the athletic model, by which the athlete is paid according to the numbers he can bring to the arena, appropriate to the church. Leaders who adopt the wrong models in the handling of money lose all credibility in the church, for the church's model was provided by the one who paid the price of serving.

The third temptation, especially for one who carries on the awesome work of the apostles before him, is the will to rule. Peter's third negative clause points to the reality of this temptation: "not as domineering over those in your charge but being examples to the flock." This advice runs like a thread through the New Testament passages on leadership. Jesus demanded a new style of leadership where men do not seek to rule over others. In the new "counter-culture" that Jesus called for, leaders would be known for their service. "You know that those who are supposed to rule over the Gentiles lord it over them, and their great men exercise authority over them. But it shall not be so among you; but whoever would be first among you must be slave of all" (Matt. 20:25-27).

Money and power may be two of the most primal temptations that drive us. Peter's advice suggests that they are also driving forces in the church, to be overcome by those who lead. Indeed, those who are shepherds of God's flock follow the model of the "chief shepherd" (5:4) who took the risks of guiding his flock. Those who lead are to be models of the Christian faith who have advanced in the Christian life.

Guidelines for Followers

Leaders are not the only ones in the Christian community who are challenged to remember that the chief shepherd calls his people to renounce the will to dominate. This will to power can be as much the temptation of those who have no power as it is of those who hold power. Thus in 1 Peter the "younger men" who are not yet prepared for leadership are also challenged to recognize that the will to rule has no place in the community. They, like others in the community (cf. 2:18; 3:1), are to recognize the value of submission (5:5), for "God opposes the proud, but gives grace to the humble."

Throughout the history of Christianity, Christian leadership has been influenced by the patterns of authority found in the wider culture. The servant leadership of early Christian communities was soon replaced by a hierarchy resembling the political establishments of the time. In the modern period, the patterns of authority are often shaped by the corporate or political world where one strives to reach the pinnacle of power. What makes leadership uniquely Christian in 1 Peter is that the whole community has learned that the drive for power has no place among those who follow the one who came to serve.

Questions for Discussion

1. Describe any changes in the leadership of the church that you have noticed in recent years. To what extent does the form of leadership inevitably become patterned after secular leadership styles?

2. Discuss the relationship between 1 Peter 4:7-11 and 5:1-5. How does the strong emphasis on mutual participation fit with the emphasis on the leadership role of the elder?

3. Discuss the comment that the church was never a democratic institution whose future was subject to the will of the majority. What is the role of the will of the people in decision-making in the church?

4. What are Peter's credentials as an elder? To what extent do we look for similar credentials in appointing elders?

5. Discuss the statement that the most fundamental task of the elder is to know and understand the Christian faith. To what extent have churches maintained this view of the elder as teacher?

6. How do the dangers of leadership mentioned in 1 Peter compare with the dangers of leadership today?

7. What are the primary ways in which money and power continue to be corrupting influences in the church?

8. First Peter accompanies advice to leaders with advice to followers. How could the church better provide teaching to the congregation on their relationship to the elders?

9. Describe the features that make leadership distinctively Christian.

Chapter 12

RESISTING OUR ADVERSARY

"Your adversary the devil prowls around like a roaring lion, seeking someone to devour."

1 Peter 5:6-11

Richard Adams' *Watership Down* tells the story of a warren of rabbits who have become refugees after signs of danger have disturbed the tranquility of their home. The rabbits love to entertain each other with stories, for stories often help them understand their world. One evening, as they are settled in for the night, one of them tells a story that they have all heard before. In the beginning, their great ancestors were strong and powerful. They were so powerful and arrogant that the lord Frith decided to do something about it. He announced one day that he would bestow gifts on all of the animal kingdom on a certain day. But he omitted to tell the great rabbit the time for the presentation. And so he passed out sharp teeth to the fox and the weasel, and eyes that can see at night to the cat. By the time the others had received their gifts, the great rabbit felt defenseless. When finally he met the lord Frith, he was desperate and afraid because he was defenseless. The lord Frith did not endow the rabbit with good offensive weapons. But he endowed him with strong feet for running and the capacity to hide. The lord Frith said, "The whole world will be your enemy, . . . and whenever they catch you they will kill you. But first they must catch you."[1] The story helped the refugee rabbits understand their situation. They lived in a hostile world, and fear was to be their constant companion.

For much of the history of Christianity, Christians have also lived in a hostile world. Totalitarians around the world have detested Christians who confessed, "Jesus Christ is Lord," for such a confession is a threat to those who claim absolute allegiance. In many places today, Christians suffer discrimination and hostility. Many faithful people became aliens in their own land during the Nazi reign of terror. Today in totalitarian societies the Christian confession renders believers vulnerable to hostile regimes. Even in modern democratic societies, the confession that "Jesus is Lord" is greeted with hostility. The confession appears to be incredibly intolerant and arrogant in a society where all claims to truth are regarded with suspicion. In this society one may be "into" Eastern religions or self-improvement, as long as no absolute claims about truth are made; but to say "Jesus is Lord" and to try to suggest that this is the one path to wholeness is to be hopelessly intolerant.

Before the era of Constantine, the Christian confession evoked hostility in the populace for very similar reasons. A society that often showed toleration toward a large number of cults was intolerant of the Christians. Christians were seen as "religious fanatics, self-righteous outsiders, arrogant innovators, who thought only their beliefs were true."[2] Among the other religions, one could belong to a variety of cults, but when one became a Christian one rejected the gods of family and neighbors. Christians were aliens in their own lands because they refused to accept the local gods. This rejection undoubtedly fueled the many rumors that the Christians were a dangerous secret society. Consequently, persecutions were often initiated by the populace, not by the magistrates. Christians were accused of "hatred of the human race."

The threat of persecution hangs over the readers of 1 Peter, as the frequent words of encouragement suggest. Some scholars have suggested that the growth of Christianity created concern among the populace, leading to sporadic outbreaks of hostility. At the beginning of the letter, we are told that the genuineness of their faith is being "tested by fire" (1:6-7). The readers are asked in 3:13, "Who is there to harm you if you are zealous for what is right?" Near the end of the letter, the prospect of suffering takes on an even more ominous tone: "Beloved, do not be surprised at the fiery ordeal which comes upon you to prove you" (4:12). The immediate future for the readers is precarious and beyond their control.

This uncertainty is the background for Peter's concluding instructions in 5:6-11. Christians must have felt that the world was their enemy and they were the prey. The anxieties mentioned in 5:7 were apparently a constant presence for the exile community. Their anxieties were probably very similar to those which are experienced by minority groups in every society. With the absence of basic human rights and the potential for job discrimination, Christians lived a vulnerable existence. They needed the resources for facing the future.

Our secular culture has its own anxieties. W. H. Auden described the twentieth century as the "age of anxiety." This anxiety is rooted in the common conviction that events are beyond our control in a world without God. First Peter reminds us that Christians have their own unique anxiety, for the faith involves risks. The believer may give up the security of fitting in with the times. The modern believer, like disciples of all ages, knows the difficulty of believing when God's power is nowhere to be seen. The forces that threaten us often seem more real than the power of God.

Cast Your Anxieties on Him

How is the Christian to cope with this anxiety? An answer is provided in the closing section of 1 Peter. The readers are told, in the first place, "Cast your anxieties on him, for he cares for you." The words remind us of Psalm 55:23,

Cast your burden on the Lord,
and he will sustain you;
he will never permit
the righteous to be moved.

A familiar theme in the New Testament is that the Christian can be liberated from anxiety. Jesus said, "Do not be anxious about your life, what you shall eat or what you shall drink, nor about your body, what you shall put on" (Matt. 6:25). Paul wrote to the Philippians, "Have no anxiety about anything, but in everything by prayer and supplication let your requests be made known to God" (Phil. 4:5). Although anxiety was the natural response for those who were asked to trust God when they could see only threats to their existence, Christians are challenged to overcome it.

How can one overcome anxiety? A simple answer is given in each of the New Testament passages. Peter says, "For he cares for you." Already he has said, "Let those who suffer according to God's will do right and entrust their souls to a faithful Creator"

(4:19). Christians have already experienced the fidelity and the love of God. They know that God cares because they have been "born again" into God's new world. They are the beneficiaries of blessings which were inaccessible even to the prophets (1:10-12)! Whenever anxiety lurks over them, they need only to recall the signs that "God cares for them."

Jesus' words about anxiety are accompanied by his reminder that the God who clothes the lilies of the field will also take care of his children (Matt. 6:25-33). Thus one does not overcome anxiety by mere willpower. Christians have seen the many signs that God cares for us. We know how the message of love has changed our own lives. At times we see his care mediated to us within the community of Christians that God has given us. We have benefited from the care of others, and our faith has given us the assurance that we are not abandoned in the universe. "God cares for us!" Behind this universe is a Father, and we have experienced his love. This knowledge gives us the strength to overcome anxiety. And therefore we "cast our cares on him" in corporate prayer. God's exiles are not alone.

In ancient times Christians were often ridiculed because of the importance that they gave to faith rather than knowledge. Their trust in a God whom they could neither see nor prove was remarkable to ancient observers. Indeed, the courage of Christians in the face of martyrdom was a common source of amazement. Christian courage came, no doubt, from the conviction that their only resource was God. They cast their cares on him in corporate prayer, "making their requests known to God" (Phil. 4:5). Even when God seemed silent, they placed their trust in him. They could trust God, even when he seemed absent, because they had already discovered his care.

Your Adversary, the Devil

The closing words of 1 Peter suggest not only that the knowl-ede of God's love is the answer for the church's anxiety. There is also a call for human effort and a reminder that the church faces a formidable adversary: "Be sober, be watchful. Your adversary the devil prowls around like a roaring lion, seeking someone to devour." The image is vivid. It reminds us of the psalmist's cry in Psalm 22:13-14,

> Many bulls encompass me,
> strong bulls of Bashan surround me;
> they open wide their mouths at me,
> like a ravening and roaring lion.

The image suggests helplessness and terror. This was the Christian life—a battle against incredible odds! The roaring lion was present in the daily lives of Christians. Behind the many adversaries who placed pressure on Christians to fit in with their environment was the one great adversary. He was the one who stood behind the persecutions, the discrimination, and the threats of violence. The experience of suffering which was afflicting the brotherhood throughout the world was nothing less than the terrifying roar of the lion. It was the source of the Christians' anxiety.

Early Christians knew that they were in a battle against an extraordinary force. "Arm yourselves," Peter says. "Resist the devil," says James (4:7). "We are not contending against flesh and blood, but against the principalities, against the world rulers of this present age, against the spiritual hosts of wickedness in the heavenly places," says Paul (Eph. 6:12ff). The devil might take many forms. He might look like the might of Rome or one of its magistrates. Wherever he was, he was the roaring lion who could cause Christians to quake with fear. Early Christians took his power seriously.

And now the Christians are being *tested* by the adversary. He pleads and entices them to give up the battle. He tests their commitment and he tells them that the price is too high. He entices them to blend in with society, to cease being an alien in their own land, to return to the festivals in honor of the gods. He challenges them to give up these things that make them so different!

Against such odds one can, of course, cast his cares on the God who cares. But the challenge demands more than God's loving care. Peter calls also for the human response: "Resist him, firm in your faith, knowing that the same experience of suffering is required of your brotherhood throughout the world." Christians are challenged to "be sober, be watchful" (5:8) and to resist the power of Satan.

The Present Danger

The early church probably did not need to be convinced of the terror of the roaring lion, for they lived in dread of its roar. To the modern reader this language appears ancient. We do not speak much of "your adversary, the devil." In the context of a Christianity that demands little, we seldom think of the Christian faith as a battle against a formidable adversary. Who comes to the pleasant surroundings of the modern church building conscious of a roaring lion who is out to devour us? And who comes thinking that the world is our enemy and we are the prey? I doubt if anyone comes expecting to hear that blood-curdling roar.

In *The Closing of the American Mind*, Allan Bloom comments that we live in a time when modern people have difficulty even using words like "good" and "evil."[3] We prefer not to speak in those terms. Our culture has replaced those ideas with the relativity of all values. To speak of the roar of the lion and the battle against evil sounds even more unthinkable to our contemporaries. We scarcely imagine a church threatened by the power of evil. What danger could possibly threaten the church as a community?

In *Watership Down* the refugee rabbits one day encounter a new warren of rabbits who appear more secure and well-fed than any they have ever seen. Here is the first group of rabbits they have known who know no danger and who do not feel that the world is its enemy. They seem to inhabit some kind of paradise, where they no longer have the most basic characteristic of all rabbits: fear. They are well fed and secure. But something is wrong. Rabbits disappear, and no one is permitted to ask where they have gone. Finally the newcomers discover the truth. This paradise is in fact the result of the farmer's realization that he does not have to keep rabbits in hutches if he fed and looked after them. He would snare a few from time to time, but not enough to frighten them away. As a result of the farmer's plan, the rabbits grew big and forgot the wild rabbit's struggle for survival. The snares were all around them, but they refuseed to talk about it. They were dying, but refused to see the danger that was destroying their community.

A church that cannot speak of "your adversary, the devil" may have much in common with the rabbits who deluded themselves into giving up their natural awareness of danger. When there is no call to "be sober, be watchful" and no call to resist the dangers to the church, one may conclude that the church is no longer engaged in a battle against a formidable adversary.

There are dangers to which one may turn a blind eye. It is possible to see no danger when in fact the roaring lion is in our midst. The church in every age faces the adversary. If he threatened the first-century church with the terror of mob action, he threatens the twentieth century with new temptations. He challenges us to adjust our message to fit the tastes of the public. We can even have growing, popular churches, if we will make few demands on our members. The adversary is there to tell us that the price of commitment is too high. He tells us to adapt, to fit in for the sake of a greater good. It is bad style to speak as if beliefs really matter. Have a message, he tells us, that is so tame that no one will be offended.

The ancient audience did not need to be convinced of the reality of the roaring lion. I suspect that we do. Indeed, many apparently successful churches may, like the well-fed and fearless rabbits of *Watership Down*, be turning a blind eye to the threats that destroy them. We may in fact look very healthy, with impressive growth and activities, and still be blind to the presence of the roaring lion.

Peter would have said to us as surely as to them: "Be sober, be watchful. . . ." The roaring lion comes to the church in all ages, testing here and there, and looking for the point of attack that is suitable for its age. There is a place for us to ask what has become of us and where we are going as a church. As with the rabbits of *Watership Down*, one resource is to be able to recognize the presence of danger.

The God of All Grace

Only those who recognize the power of the roaring lion can appreciate the promise that follows the warning. "And after you have suffered for a little while, the God of all grace, who has called you to his eternal glory in Christ, will himself restore, establish and strengthen you." The exiles appear to be no match for the roaring lion. But the exiles are protected by "the God of all grace." Those who have no resources of their own can depend on the God whose strength far surpasses that of the roaring lion. On the basis of what God has done in the past, we believe that he has given us a future. The story in which we are involved will turn out contrary to all appearances because of God. "To him be dominion for ever and ever."

NOTES

1 Cf. Stanley Hauerwas, *A Community of Character: Toward a Constructive Christian Social Ethic* (London: Notre Dame, 1981), 15ff.

2 Robert L. Wilken, *The Christians as the Romans Saw Them* (New Haven: Yale University Press, 1984), 63.

3 Allan Bloom, *The Closing of the American Mind: How Higher Education Has Failed Democracy and Impoverished the Souls of Today's Students* (New York: Simon & Schuster, 1987), 142.

Questions for Discussion

1. Why has the Christian claim, "Jesus is Lord," always been offensive, both to democratic and totalitarian societies? Discuss whether this claim is actually offensive in American society. Under what conditions?

2. Examine the references in 1 Peter to the hostility of the neighbors. What form did the hostility take? Overt persecution by government authorities? Occasional mob violence? Discrimination?

3. Compare the anxiety of our time with the anxiety described in 1 Peter and elsewhere in the New Testament. What is the New Testament advice for responding to anxiety?

4. Discuss the comment that the devil, who appears very real in 1 Peter, is seldom discussed today. Have we lost something very important in our not discussing the devil?

5. First Peter strongly emphasizes ideas about "being watchful" because of the strength of the enemy. Have we seen dangers on two sides? Of those who saw the "enemy" everywhere? And of those who saw him nowhere? How can the church find the right balance?

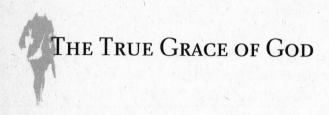
THE TRUE GRACE OF GOD

"I have written briefly to you, exhorting and declaring that this is
the true grace of God."

1 Peter 5:12-14

In 1896 Charles Sheldon wrote a popular novel that was to
become a classic statement of the religious values of millions
of Americans of that period. The novel was entitled *In His Steps*,
and it has sold more than thirty million copies since its first
printing. It has been translated into more than twenty languages.
The novel is set in Raymondville, U.S.A., where a congregation
is shaken one day by the tragic death of an unemployed printer
seeking help. The minister and the rest of the congregation are
so moved by the experience that their Christian discipleship
was transformed. Casual churchgoing was replaced by attempts
at showing authentic discipleship. Everyone began to focus his
life around the question: What would Jesus do? That question
challenged the predominant view of Christianity and brought
about a revolution within the entire church. The book follows
the path of several members of the congregation as they confront

the question, What would Jesus do? All of the church members discover that following in the steps of Jesus is more demanding than the expected routine of church life.

This discovery has been made by many others who were confronted with the words of Jesus. Jesus' call, "Follow me," was accompanied by the rigorous demands for taking up a cross (Mark 8:34), abandoning one's family (Luke 9:60; cf. Luke 14:25), one's occupation (cf. Mark 1:18), and one's wealth (Mark 10:21). Indeed, the disciples comment that they have "left all"—family, lands, property—to follow Jesus (Mark 10:28). From the first century to the twentieth century, these disturbing words of Jesus have impacted Christians, convincing them that Christ demands more than the "cheap grace" of a domesticated Christianity. In 1940 those words had such an impact on Dietrich Bonhoeffer that he left the safety of his teaching position in New York to return to his native Germany, where he worked against the Nazis until he was arrested and executed. The call to discipleship has had its impact on other heroic individuals.

Jürgen Moltmann once commented that the language of discipleship has been the preserve of fanatics. The churches preferred a less demanding form of Christianity that offered grace at little cost. Sheldon's book, *In His Steps*, was not acclaimed as a very good novel, but it did confront millions of people with the demands of discipleship. The title of the book was taken from 1 Peter 2:21, "For to this you have been called, because Christ also suffered for you, leaving you an example, that you should follow *in his steps*." This advice to Christian slaves in 1 Peter is the heart of the epistle, for the advice extends to all Christians to follow in the steps of Jesus. This epistle grapples with what it means for the whole church to follow Jesus "in his steps." Indeed, the epistle reminds us that the call to discipleship was meant, not for a few heroic individuals, but for an entire community.

What does it mean to follow in his steps? While no one disputes the claim of 1 Peter that Christians follow in the steps of Jesus, we face an incredible variety of answers when we ask what it means. For millions in the Western world, following Jesus involves turning to a church community for a blessing at the major transitional moments of their lives. I was told of a local church parish in Germany where a questionnaire was sent to the local populace asking each household if they were still members of the state church. Unless people responded otherwise, they would be considered church members and left on the church rolls. The church was the place for baptisms, weddings, funerals, and other special occasions. In America, the majority of the population follows Jesus, according to the Gallup polls. For more than fifteen hundred years we have seen a Christian culture where following Jesus involved few demands and little change in people's lives. Grace has been offered without discipleship.

The True Grace of God

When 1 Peter comes to a close, the content of the entire book is summarized in 5:12: "By Silvanus, a faithful brother as I regard him, I have written briefly to you, exhorting and declaring that this is the true grace of God; stand fast in it." That is, 1 Peter is an epistle about the grace of God. It is a very short epistle, and the writer correctly says that he has written briefly. Perhaps Silas, who had earlier been Paul's companion, had acted either as a scribe or deliverer of the letter. The letter is, undoubtedly, what the writer would have said if he had been there. He has written both to *encourage* and to *testify* (NIV) to a community that could easily have felt abandoned and hopeless because of the constant pressure of living the Christian life surrounded by ridicule and hostility. As aliens and exiles, they had found it costly to follow Jesus, and thus they needed these words of encouragement and witness.

If the readers felt abandoned in a hopeless situation, they could have wondered if the grace of God was absent from their lives. If Christians could have pointed to prosperity or visible success in their ministry, they might easily have pointed to the acts of God's grace and to the power of his presence. If they had seen signs of victory in their mission, the presence of God's grace would not have been doubted. But in their difficult circumstances, the presence of God's grace was open to question.

The content of the entire book is summarized with the declaration that "this is the *true* grace of God in which you stand." Others might claim to experience God's grace, but these isolated Christians, in their difficult circumstances, were experiencing the *true* grace of God in the midst of suffering.

Most readers would summarize the content of 1 Peter in terms of its attention to the innocent suffering by Christians, who live as "exiles" (1:1; 2:11) in a hostile environment. The pervasive theme is the suffering of the Christian (cf. 2:19, 20; 3:14; 4:15, 16; 5:9, 10), whose faith is now being tested (cf. 1:6-7). The evidence of 1 Peter suggests that Christians suffer more from slander and discrimination than from any physical suffering. This experience, according to 5:12, is "the true grace of God." The epistle is written to tell suffering Christians that the grace of God is experienced, not in times of success and ease, but at the very moments when their faith is being tested. If they had felt abandoned by God, they are told that they now stand in the grace of God (5:12) when they seem weak, vulnerable, and defenseless.

What does it mean to follow Jesus? To walk "in his steps," according to 1 Peter, means to share the suffering of Jesus (4:13). Christians are reminded repeatedly in 1 Peter that, before they were rejected, Christ was the rejected one (2:4-10). When Christian slaves suffer unjustly, they recall that Christ went before them. When the whole community suffers for righteousness' sake, they recall that Jesus Christ preceded them in suffering (cf. 3:17-22). But then they are reminded that the suffering of Jesus ended in victory (3:18-22), for the one who was rejected now sits at the right hand of God. God's grace was present in the suffering of his people.

A Costly Victory

This sense of victory explains why 1 Peter is not characterized by despair, but by hope and joy (cf. 1:3, 13, 21; 3:15 on hope; cf. 1:6; 4:13 on joy). The readers are not the victims of unfortunate circumstances as they live the exile existence. They are in fact following in the steps of Jesus on a path that leads to victory. They, and not their neighbors, are the recipients of the true grace of God.

At some periods in the history of Christianity this message has spoken with special power, while at other times the epistle has been an almost forgotten book. We noticed in chapter 1 that the epistle spoke with great force to those who attempted to walk "in his steps" in a totalitarian society. The epistle's message of encouragement helped many people discover that the "true grace of God" is to be discovered when we must depend absolutely on it.

During the Nazi occupation of Norway, the Nazis imprisoned Eivind Berggrav, a leading churchman, because he spoke out against the regime. When he felt the persecution of the Nazis, he once said, "Have you noticed how full of life the Bible has become, as if written for people in war and during times of occupation?"[1]

One book that spoke to him in a special way was 1 Peter. As he was led to prison, he took out his New Testament and read from 1 Peter 3:15: "Have no fear of them, nor be troubled, but in your hearts reverence Christ as Lord." He found special encouragement—the true grace of God—in reading 1 Peter.

Whenever Christians have forgotten that walking in the steps of Jesus is costly, 1 Peter has been a forgotten book. The "true grace of God" hardly seems necessary for communities which are rich with their own resources. Where membership in the family of God is offered at bargain-basement prices, the message of 1 Peter is sure to be irrelevant, for only alien communities will find that this book still speaks a word of encouragement.

The contemporary church is faced with a crisis of identity as it faces the changes that have taken place in our culture. In *The Next Christendom*, Philip Jenkins has demonstrated that Christianity is literally "going south,"[2] marking one of the great transitions in the history of Christianity. Whereas Christianity was once identified with Europe and North America, its center in the coming years will be the southern hemisphere. While we may regard the explosive growth of Christianity in Asia and the southern hemisphere with enthusiasm, we confront the problem of the decline of the "Christian society" often described as "Christendom."

Many Christians maintain that the church's task is to take the steps that will ensure the popularity of Christianity in our society. Neil Postman, in *Amusing Ourselves to Death*, has described the dilemma which faces those who communicate the gospel to this secular culture. In his chapter entitled, "Shuffling Off to Bethlehem," he notes that popular religious broadcasters have no message of discipleship, for their task is to attract people. In some of the most successful religious programs, the need to attract the

151

audience requires exotic locations, handsome personalities (celebrities, if possible), and sophisticated marketing procedures. He says, "the preachers are forthright about how they control the content of their preaching to maximize their ratings."[3] The executive director of the National Religious Broadcasters Association sums up what he calls the unwritten law of religious broadcasters: "You can get your share of the audience only by offering people something they want."[4] Where the people are offered what they want, the call to follow Jesus "in his steps" is not heard. Instead, what is offered is affluence, peace of mind, and other items on the perceived wish list of the viewers. It is a world far removed from 1 Peter, where "the true grace of God" is costly and demanding.

Peter's challenge to "stand fast" (5:12) in this grace is a challenge not only to the residents of ancient Asia Minor, but to the contemporary church as well. Christianity began as an unpopular minority movement. When the church maintained its identity, it made an impression on the wider populace. The proper role of the church in a secular culture is not to offer the populace what it wants, but to follow the path of the rejected one who gave himself for others.

A Worldwide Fellowship (5:13)

The communities undoubtedly found strength to stand apart from their societies in those house churches where they knew that they had a place to belong. The opening words of 1 Peter indicate that they could even find strength in the knowledge that their situation was shared by Christians in Pontus, Galatia, Cappadocia, Asia, and Bithynia. In 5:9, they are challenged to endure their situation, "knowing that the same experience of suffering is required of your brotherhood throughout the world." Even without the modern means of communication, local house churches knew that they belonged to a brotherhood which was located "throughout the world." The closing words of 1 Peter also provide a reminder of this worldwide brotherhood: "She who is at Babylon, who is likewise chosen, sends you greetings; and so does my son Mark" (5:13).

The "Babylon" of 1 Peter is apparently Rome, as the references to Babylon in the book of Revelation suggest (Rev. 14:8; 16:19; 17:5; 18:2). The final greeting indicates the strong bonds that connect not only Peter and Mark to the churches in this distant region, but the bonds that brought churches together as well. At the beginning of the letter, the exile recipients of 1 Peter are called God's "chosen" (or "elect") ones. At the conclusion of the letter they are reminded that they have brothers and sisters who are "likewise chosen" by God. While they are separated from their families and neighbors, they are united with Christians who live thousands of miles away.

Ancient people would have been amazed to see the ties of solidarity which connected Christians in distant lands. The writers of the letters of the New Testament routinely add their greetings at the end of the letters. These greetings are often accompanied by the greetings of Christians in the local church where the writer is staying. The author of Hebrews concludes his letter, "Greet all your leaders and all the saints. Those who come from Italy send you greetings" (13:24). Paul concludes Philippians, "The brethren who are with me greet you" (3:21). In Romans, the scribe says, "I Tertius, the writer of this letter, greet you in the Lord." Then follow greetings from Gaius, Paul's host, Erastus, the city treasurer, and Quartus (16:23). Both 1 and 2 Corinthians conclude with greetings from the church in Asia. We do not know what past relationships lie behind these greetings. In many instances, Christians knew their brethren in distant lands from their frequent travels. In other instances, they knew them from reports that they received. While they could not have known each other well, they found in Jesus Christ the bonds that united them.

The contemporary church could be strengthened enormously if Christians recognized that our community includes not only God's chosen ones in the local congregation, but the many who are "likewise chosen" (1 Pet. 5:13) in our own cities and in distant lands. Congregations are united by the same confession of faith, and together they are shaped by the same story of the one who was rejected by his contemporaries.

Today local churches sometimes appeal to the consumer mentality of the people, entering into competition with other congregations. Under these circumstances church growth is reduced to gaining a competitive edge with other Christian communities. The competitive edge is not likely to come from calling a community to be a holy people, but from demanding less. Where we seek this competitive edge, our concern is only with the health of our own community. In extreme situations, churches grow at the expense of other churches, even finding satisfaction in the misfortunes of other communities. In 1 Peter, local communities of Christians regard distant communities as members of the same family. They are brought together by their common choice to walk in the steps of Jesus.

Today the task for the church is not to become more popular to a secular society, but to be faithful to its commitment. We will discover that "the true grace of God" is to be found in being God's "counterculture." As in the late first century, it is no unfortunate circumstance if Christians are exiles in their own land. Our story did not begin with a popular Savior, but with one whose people did not receive him. The place for his people is to follow "in his steps."

NOTES

1   Carl E. Braaten, *Stewards of the Mysteries: Sermons for Festivals and Special Occasions* (Minneapolis: Augsburg, 1983), 98.
2   Philip Jenkins, *The Next Christendom: The Coming of Global Christianity* (New York: Oxford, 2002), 3.
3   Neil Postman, *Amusing Ourselves to Death: Public Discourse in the Age of Show Business* (New York: Penguin, 1984), 121.
4   Quoted in ibid.

Questions for Discussion

1. Discuss instances in the history of Christianity where Jesus' call to follow him resulted in extraordinary sacrifice. Is it true that discussion of discipleship is a forgotten topic in many churches? Explain.

2. First Peter is summarized with the words: "This is the true grace of God." Discuss the difference between the concept of the grace of God in 1 Peter and in our normal discussion of the topic. Compare the "true grace" with "cheap grace."

3. Under what circumstances is 1 Peter likely to be a forgotten book?

4. Discuss the most frequent advertisements you have seen from churches. What role does the cost of discipleship

play? What reasons are commonly given for one to become a church member? How does this message compare with 1 Peter?

5. Discuss the significance that 1 Peter places on a worldwide fellowship, indicating the importance of the wider brotherhood for our Christian life. Compare the sense of brotherhood and "connectedness" reflected in 1 Peter with our own emphasis on the wider fellowship. How is the wider fellowship important to us?

Also Available

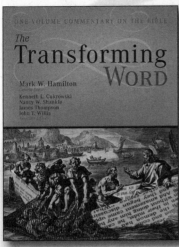

The Transforming Word
One Volume Commentary on the Bible

General Editor

Mark W. Hamilton
(Ph.D., Harvard University),
Associate Professor of Old Testament,
Abilene Christian University

Associate Editors

Kenneth L. Cukrowski (Ph.D., Yale University)
Nancy W. Shankle (Ph.D., Texas A & M University)
James W. Thompson (Ph.D., Vanderbilt University)
John T. Willis (Ph.D., Vanderbilt University)

1136 pages, $69.95 cloth
ISBN 978-0-112-521-1

This volume contains a commentary on each book of the Bible. The reader should expect to gain an understanding of (1) the organization and arguments of each biblical book, (2) the main historical issues bearing on its interpretation, and (3) the theological meaning of each book. It also includes additional articles on the background of the Old and New Testaments.

"*The Transforming Word* is a wonderful guide for all serious readers of Holy Scripture. There is a clear exposition of each book of the Bible enabling the student to see interweaving themes and the overarching unity of God's written word. A great resource for the church!"

—TIMOTHY GEORGE, founding dean of Beeson Divinity School, Samford University

"The editors and authors should be commended for their work on this milestone publishing event. . . . a valuable addition to anyone's library, particularly someone who does not have a commentary on every book of the Bible."

—TERRY BRILEY, Dean, College of Bible and Ministry, Lipscomb University, Nashville, Tennessee

An ideal reference tool for small group Bible study leaders,
adult Sunday School teachers, preaching ministers, elders,
and all serious students of the Scriptures

1-877-816-4455 toll free
www.abilenechristianuniversitypress.com

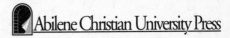
Abilene Christian University Press

THE MEDITATIVE COMMENTARY SERIES

An exciting new Bible study tool for small groups

Twelve volumes covering the New Testament.

MATTHEW
Jesus Is King
Gary Holloway
224 pages $13.99
ISBN 978-0-9767790-1-8

MARK
Jesus Is God's Son
Earl Lavender
144 pages $11.99
ISBN 978-0-89112-551-8

LUKE
Jesus Is Savior
Earl Lavender
240 pages $13.99
ISBN 978-0-89112-500-6

JOHN
Believing in Jesus
Gary Holloway
144 pages $10.99
ISBN 978-0-89112-504-4

ACTS OF THE APOSTLES
Jesus Alive
in His Church
Earl Lavender
224 pages $13.99
ISBN 978-0-89112-501-3

ROMANS & GALATIANS
The Spirit of Jesus
Gary Holloway
144 pages $11.99
ISBN 978-0-89112-502-0

1 & 2 CORINTHIANS
Jesus, Cross, Church
Earl Lavender
144 pages $11.99
ISBN 978-0-89112-568-6

**EPHESIANS,
PHILIPPIANS,
COLOSSIANS, &
PHILEMON**
Jesus Above All
Earl Lavender
112 pages $9.99
ISBN 978-0-89112-561-7

**1 & 2 THESSALONIANS,
1 & 2 TIMOTHY, TITUS**
Jesus Grows
His Church
Gary Holloway
128 pages $11.99
ISBN 978-0-89112-503-7

HEBREWS & JAMES
Brother Jesus
Gary Holloway
112 pages $10.99
ISBN 978-0-89112-505-1

**THE LETTERS OF
PETER, JOHN,
& JUDE**
Living in Jesus
Gary Holloway
96 pages $8.99
ISBN 978-0-89112-557-0

REVELATION
Jesus the
Conquering Lamb
Terry Briley
128 pages $10.99
ISBN 978-0-89112-559-4

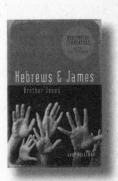

All titles are

6 x 9 · trade paper · Biblical Reference